Y0-BCF-785

B. B. Bailey

Shelbyville

Ky.

1920

EDUCATIONAL EVANGELISM

The Religious Discipline for Youth

BY
CHARLES E. McKINLEY

———

BOSTON
The Pilgrim Press
NEW YORK   CHICAGO

*

To
Isaac   Addison   McKinley
and
Mary Allspaugh McKinley
in token of a
Son's Imperishable Love.

Preface

THE following essay endeavors to develop, briefly and suggestively, a conception of the religious discipline that is to be regarded as most fitting and desirable for the years of adolescence in view of the spiritual experiences through which nature conducts the young soul on the road to maturity. The standpoint is not that of an expert scientific investigator, but that of one bound to a goodly company of youth by ties of personal sympathy. The writer has done his best, however, for their sakes, to profit by the scientific investigation of the phenomena of youth, and his indebtedness to all those who, in recent years, have written so ably upon adolescence and religious psychology—Hall, James, Starbuck, Coe, Granger, and many more—is manifest on every page. Not so manifest, perhaps, but quite as worthy of acknowledgment, are his obligations to the remarkable book by Charles Wagner entitled " Youth," to which he owes some of the initial insights of this study.

He ventures, however, to presume that the reader will be able to discern, without the aid of further acknowledgments, the extent of these various obligations, and to judge for himself whether, deducting the evident liabilities, there remain in the volume any net assets of sound thinking or suggestive insight. He is guilty also of presuming that the standpoint which he occupies may furnish something worth saying, even to one all inexpert in the methods of the laboratory and the use of the questionnaire. Love is sometimes more penetrating than research, and things have been revealed to babes that were not discovered by the wise and prudent. And if it should be said that in forsaking the methods of exact science to follow the guidance of sympathetic insight, the author is turning from the light of day to wander in the dark, his sufficient consolation would be the fact that night also has its wonderful disclosures, for then

" The sky is filled with stars, invisible by day."

NOTE.—Chapter III reproduces some of the thought and language of an address at the Bushnell Centennial in Hartford in 1902, published in the commemorative volume. Chapter VIII likewise contains the substance of an address published in *Men of To-morrow* for January, 1901. Both chapters are wholly different in conception, plan and development from the addresses out of which they grew.

Contents

EDUCATIONAL EVANGELISM

CHAPTER I

An Introduction to Youth

"I WOULD there were no age between sixteen and three-and-twenty, or that youth would sleep out the rest!"

It is one of the imperishable memories of college days. The professor in the Shakespeare class was calling for choice passages from a play assigned for private reading, a bland smile playing over his features as we gave our patronizing approval to this and that specimen of the great dramatist's work, varied, however, now and then, with a snap of the eyes that threatened to break his glasses.

Did I overestimate the personal tone that my classmate put into these words which he quoted, as if they expressed his views exactly? Possibly; for I, too, was sick of being a boy, eager to be a man. And I was half convinced—what youth is not?—that all professors and older people generally cherish a lurking approval of the shepherd's maledictory wish.

For is not youth the troublesome age? Is it not the self-conceited, smart, restless, wayward, rebellious age, the age for which mature people have least sympathy, of which youth itself has most dread? And is not the keenest pain of youth just this, that while the grown folks may find it uncomfortable to have a big boy in the house, they do not seem to understand that it is many times more uncomfortable to be the big boy?

What is youth? A wide, deep river, dividing childhood from manhood; a river which, like the river of death, must be crossed without bridge or boat; *through* which each soul must go; into whose turbid waters the child must descend alone, knowing well that beneath their flood his childhood will be buried to rise no more; a stream both broad and turbulent, not to be crossed in a day or a year; whose buoyant waters will indeed bear him up, but not without his efforts; whose currents will land him somewhere on the other shore, but, oh, so far down stream, on the dusty plains of sordid, sinful manhood, far out of sight of those green hills of childhood that were so near to heaven.

Only by some such figure can we picture to ourselves this wide interval between the child and the man. It is a time when all is fluid, restless, changing, nothing settled or fixed, no foundation sure; when one is carried off his feet, away from the moorings of early years, and swept towards he knows not what destiny by strange, new currents of life that he does not comprehend; a fascinating, wondrous time of freshness and bloom, when unmeasured continents of power are discovered in the soul, opening up boundless possibilities, and new visions of life and its meaning come sweeping daily before the spirit's eyes as one is borne along to viewpoints ever new; a time of exhilaration and suspense, while forces of nature beyond control rush one forward in the resistless progress toward a goal that is hidden as yet from sight.

Youth has been maligned; because it is easier for Shakespeare's shepherd—and others—to grumble than to understand.

For the fact is that youth is still the portion of human life least understood. Lovers of children are we all, but downright lovers of youth are few. The dullest heart responds to the appeal of childhood, but only the discerning kindle at contact with youth. The last century was the children's era. Child-life has had its prophets and interpreters. Froebel and Robert Raikes and Horace Bushnell and Horace Mann have had a multitude of followers. The study of the child's mind has been exalted to a science; the interests of childhood have been amply set forth, its rights ably defended; elementary education has been revolutionized, and the world has been led at last to a respectable understanding of the needs and nature of the child.

But many of the phenomena of youth are still regarded with uncomprehending amazement. The attitude of the majority toward youth is about this: "Childhood we know, and manhood we know; but who, or what, art thou?" The largest part of mankind is waiting for an introduction to youth; they are still strangers after all. But there are those who are seeking an acquaintance in all seriousness. They no longer assume that they know youth. Youth is no longer to be taken for granted and ignored. The inductive study of the mind and spirit of youth is being pursued with a zeal that is according to knowledge and a zest that falters at no difficulty or magnitude in the work to be done. Many influences have conspired to bring the interests and problems of youthful life before the world as never before. The study of the mind of the child was certain to lead, in time, to more thorough investigation of the special characteristics of youth; the development of primary education made imperative a reformation of secondary education, which in turn called for a better understanding of the native interests and essential needs of those in the formative period of adolescence; the rapid rise of young people's religious societies compelled thoughtful attention to the serious problems which they raised; and expert scientists have already done an epoch-making work to promote a better understanding of the mind of youth.

The unique and distinctive character of this period, the nature of the process by which the child becomes a man, the order of development and the character of the successive changes that take place, are now defined with far greater precision than ever before. The way is clear for that better acquaintance with youth which is in every way so desirable. Our present purpose is to look into the naturally ordered spiritual experience of youth, and seek therein for hints to help in the religious treatment of those who are passing through these restless years. The effort can hardly be fruitless; and it will be richly worth while if it should lead some who are impatient with the ways of youth to repent of having ever wished that there were no age between sixteen and three-and-twenty.

By the spiritual experience of youth we are to understand that inward experience, howsoever affected by influences from without, by which a personal character is formed.

The formation of his individual, personal character is the supreme work of youth. The method may be that of the natural unfolding of the character implicit in his childhood's virtues, or that of personal enrichment in character through entrance into a more complex life, or that of the radical alteration of character to suit a changed environment as he passes from youth to manhood, or that of a revolution that changes his character for good or ill at all its cardinal points in a day ; in any case, the business of character-forming is youth's greatest concern, and the character with which he issues into the field of manhood is his best capital or his heaviest drag in later life.

Now the process of character-formation is not to be viewed apart from the other interests and tasks of youth. It goes hand in hand with the transformation of the child in body, mind and spirit into a man. At every stage it is profoundly influenced, where it is not actually controlled, by the factors then dominant in the general process. The entire process of transformation extends over a period of ten or a dozen years, from the age of thirteen onward, beginning and ending earlier, as everybody knows, with girls than with boys. Within these years a certain order of development is practically universal, making possible a division of youth itself into three distinct periods. The beginning and ending of these periods are not at all distinctly marked, nor are the interests of one excluded from the others; yet the special character of each is plain. If we divide the entire time between the end of childhood and the beginning of maturity into three nearly equal periods, and call the first the physical, the second the mental, and the third the social period of adolescence, we shall have a rough framework for our study, a broad outline which is yet accurate enough for our present general purpose.

In the first of these periods, say from the thirteenth to the seventeenth year, the formation of character is profoundly influenced by bodily growth. It is the time of most rapid, often of sudden and surprising, physical development. Growth is often dispropor-

tionate, and size comes faster than strength.
When a boy suddenly shoots up tall and slen-
der, with shoulders too narrow for his height
and hands and feet too large for the limbs
that carry them, and all his frame loose in
the joints, how could it be possible for him
to display the moral character or have the
spiritual experiences of a curly-headed,
round-faced child, or of a well-knit man?
The development of the physical differences
in the sexes in this period is accompanied
by the appearance of marked differences in
their mental and moral natures. When we
remember that " the hot blood of youth " is
not a figure of speech but a literal fact, the
temperature of the body in adolescence being about a degree higher than in earlier or
later years, we should know better than to
expect from the youth either the quiet sub-
missiveness of the child or the cool judgment of the man. When we think how
nature dowers youth with seemingly inexhaustible supplies of new energy, repairing
all their prodigal waste with lavish hand, so
that they rush into exhausting contests and
foolhardy adventures with undoubting as-

surance of their ability to make good all losses, we are not so much surprised that they should take, without a thought of danger, moral risks that to older heads are simply appalling. And when we reflect that, do the best she can, nature cannot transform the body of a boy into that of a man in less than ten years' time, we may be disposed to exercise more patience with the seemingly slow progress of our young people in moral and spiritual attainment.

Mental development is rapid from the beginning of youth, and physical development is not complete until the end of the period; but as rapid physical growth dominates the early, so rapid mental growth dominates the middle years of adolescence. The unfolding of the mental powers is even more intimately associated with the development of character than physical growth. The larger mental vision requires a readjustment of the ideals of life. The youth begins to reason, to follow intricate and elaborate processes of argument, to form judgments based on a more and more extended view of facts and principles. Delighting in his independence of thought, he takes pleasure in questioning the wisdom of others, and in confuting their statements. He shapes his own convictions, and often shows a greater confidence in his own conclusions than their merit warrants. The kindling of imagination places before his mind a set of ideals and ambitions, self-discovered and self-chosen, which henceforth dominate the moral and spiritual movements of his being. The emotional awakening that accompanies this increase of mental breadth and reach is also of vast significance for character. That disturbance of the emotional equilibrium, that agitation of a soul dragged hither and thither by conflicting impulses and desires, which is known as the "storm and stress" of the spirit, now reaches its height. The youth who as a child was entertained with hero tales, admired the heroes and dreaded the villains, now feels it in himself to be in very truth, not in childish play, a hero or a villain, or both. His intensified self-consciousness makes him by turns bashful and bold, diffident and boastful, secretive and assertive. With overweening sense of the value of his new-found personal self, he may become heartlessly selfish ; or the altruistic feelings may win dominion over him, and make him more than ever a loving son, a devoted brother, a generous friend.

But the full dominance of the altruistic feelings belongs to the last or social period of youth. That is the time when one finds his place and settles to his work in the world, when the life reaches out beyond oneself and he learns to know himself as a factor in the life of the community, when he enters responsibly upon his social and civic duties as a citizen. The social impulse that rules this time is, of course, most conspicuously displayed in the relations of the sexes. In early adolescence the boys and girls part company by instinct; totally diverse interests come to control the two sexes for a time. But in the social period there is a gradual return to common interests and mutual understanding, to likeness of tastes and feelings, an approach that culminates in the love-making and the mating of young men and women to create new social centers in homes of their own. All this cannot but

have much to do with the inner spiritual
experience that finally issues in a settled
character. It is to be certainly expected
that altruistic and social considerations will
now exert great influence on the process of
character-formation, and that the rise of
the social instincts to controlling power, and
the adjustment of young lives to their place
and work in the world, will be accompanied
by marked decisions and significant defini-
tions that go far to give personal character
its final form.

This introduction to the distinctive interests of the different periods of youth is
sufficient to show that the spiritual experience of youth must be something great and
deep and infinitely varied. He who would
explore it will be led into a forest wide and
dark, which is for some a wilderness, with
many a bog and fen, and many a trackless
waste. Many and devious are the paths
that lead through it, highways and byways
of the soul in its journey from childhood to
maturity; uncharted mostly, and some un-
traversed save by one who goes his way

alone. Yet all these myriad paths, these countless forms of experience, despite their infinite variety, have one general trend; they all lead through the forest; by this way or by that, with many turnings or with few, the youth emerges at last from the forest shades into the broad light of manhood's open plain.

Our next step, therefore, will be the endeavor to sketch an outline map of the journey as a whole. Ignoring the fascinating details of the personal adventures of individual travelers through this forest, we shall note the general trend of their various paths, mark the points that all must pass, and observe the places of peculiar danger or promise. In other words, we shall attempt a general outline of the typical, essential, spiritual experiences through which we are to expect the youth to pass on his way from childhood to maturity, and in which the laws of his spiritual education are to be discerned.

CHAPTER II

The Drama of Youth

DURING the years that divide childhood from maturity, there is enacted in the soul a drama second to none in significance and interest. To understand this drama is to acquire a deeper, wiser love for youth. To sketch it in outline, setting forth the normal sequence of spiritual experiences through which the youth is conducted in the course of his development, is the object of this chapter.

In the transformation of the child into the man, there are three great things to be done. We observe, accordingly, three acts in the drama of youth. They correspond also in a general way with the three periods of adolescence. The dramatic action of the first period centers in the youth's achievement of his personal freedom; in the second, in his discovery of life; in the third, in his incorporation, as a distinct individual,

25

into the social body. The first step to a
sympathetic understanding of youth is an
intelligent acquaintance with the necessary,
dramatic action within the spirit by which
these successive objects are attained.

How, then, does the soul achieve its freedom ? How does the child set out to become a man ?

The child is born into a ready-made
world, and spends his childhood in becoming familiar with it. By it he is sustained,
protected, instructed. To it he conforms, in
most instances willingly, in exceptional ones
under stress of discipline. But before the
child can be a man, he must work this
ready-made world over into the terms of his
personal life ; for every man must, in a sense,
build his own world. When therefore the
child becomes a youth he casts off the world
that he has known, like so many pieces of
clothing outgrown. He begins to build his
own world. He begins to act on his own
initiative, rather than at the command of
others. He feels new powers at work
within him, preparing him to be independent
of support and control. As he becomes too

large in body to be governed by corporal
punishment, and strong enough to be effective at manual labor or manly sports, his
mind also refuses control from without and
displays a new. efficiency in independent
work. He can think more surely, see more
deeply, comprehend more widely; and
withal he is conscious of a new constructive
power to form and execute his own designs.
All this unsettles his relation to his world;
the physical uneasiness of the period is
matched by mental and spiritual unrest.

The ready-made world of custom, rule and
convention is now required to justify itself
to the mind of the youth; and if it be not
founded on the everlasting rocks, he will
find it out, and go delving for a better
foundation. In order to make a man of
him, nature draws him apart, bids him ex-
amine and make sure of his foundations,
sets him over against his entire environment, and makes him doubt and question
and criticize that world in which he finds
himself. As a child, he was in and of that
world; now he comes to regard himself as
apart from it. He no longer relies on it for

support or defense. He often feels himself
alone, with battles to fight in which assistance from without is impossible; yet even
so feels proudly conscious that he is strong
enough to fight and win. A spirit of self-
sufficiency is awake within him. The wisdom of his parents is no longer wise enough
for him, and the truth of his teachers no
longer true enough for him, and the God of
his church no longer great enough for him.
The new life that animates him requires
him to stand apart from it all as a separate
individual. Habits, thoughts, places, activities, and even persons that have been his
delight now lose their attractions for him.
In a word, the soul of the youth is alienated
from its world.

It is by such alienation that the soul
achieves its freedom. The child setting out
to become a man must be expected to find
himself in frequent opposition to his childhood's world of ideas, habits and purposes,
to cease to be confiding and submissively
obedient, and to seek his law within. Such
an alienation of spirit, much more pronounced in some cases than in others, is a

normal characteristic of youth. One investigator found that ninety per cent of the young people whom he studied loved solitude. The reason is apparent: estrangement is the price the soul must pay for individuality. Before the soul is fitted for the activities of a man's life, it must needs retire upon itself, separate itself from the world, from customs and regulations that have been familiar, get its own point of view, and estimate the worth of things for itself. It is in seclusion that the soul comes to know its own freedom, works its ideas and convictions into a harmony, forms its great life purposes, and becomes really able to stand alone before the world. Like the Prodigal Son, the soul must gather all its own together and withdraw to a far country; but it is not prodigals only that do so; before entering upon life's work, Moses and Elijah, Christ and Paul, went alone into the wilderness.

The second act in the drama of youth is the discovery of life. Going forth master of himself and of his own affairs, the youth makes trial of life on his own responsibility. He "sees life"; he discovers what life is; and his first discovery is tragic.

The tragedy of human life is this: that while none can be a man until his soul has achieved its freedom, yet none is wise enough to make faultless use of freedom when secured. Man is no sooner free than he becomes a sinner. Since the world began, says one, there has never been a child but was told that if he played with the fire he would be burned; and since the world began there has never been a child but has played with the fire and been burned. Among the experiences that are universal and seem to be necessary for the realization of our human estate, that of being burned with fire and that of being singed with sin must be reckoned.

We have seen that the soul comes to know its own liberty by setting itself over against all else, questioning the conventional order of the ready-made world in which it finds itself, and seeking its own foundations on which to build the structure of its own life. Such an alienation is a necessary step on the road to individual completeness; it is the true self-assertion, in which the soul definitely proposes to itself to go about its essential business of ordering its own life. But new discoveries are commonly exaggerated; they fill the field of vision and exclude all else from sight. When the soul of youth comes to feel its duty to be an individual self, it is almost certain to overestimate the amount of self-assertion needful. The necessary assertion of self in contrast with the external world, by an easy and natural exaggeration, passes over into an obstinate refusal to learn from others or be guided by their experience, or leads to an unwillingness to recognize the validity of any standard of obligation outside one's self. This is self-will, the enthronement of youth's poor, inexperienced self, as the only authority, the monarch of his world. And herein is sin.

The classical picture of the exaggerated self-will of youth is, of course, the parable of the Prodigal Son. Its present interest for us lies in its lively depicting of the consequences of extravagant self-will.

Rioting in the excesses of new-found freedom, the Prodigal doubtless believed that he was seeing life: and so he was—one part of it. In the days of swine-feeding and starvation he saw the rest. And then he saw the whole at once. And this is the discovery that youth is to make, that life is a whole, all its parts bound inseparably together; that every deed shall have its effect on the doer, every act shall be registered indelibly upon the soul of him that does it, there to bear its eternal witness to what he has been and is. No warning or counsel, nothing but experience, will teach this lesson to most young men. "Whatsoever a man soweth, that shall he also reap," is an authentic statement of Holy Writ; but no youth really believes it until he begins to reap some harvest from his own sowing. Hosts of youth, going forth to see life for themselves, do not understand that the fruit of extravagance is want, that indulgence leads to weakness, that to squander money or strength or character must bring one, by a law as changeless as the course of the sun, to poverty of resources, or power, or morals.

It often takes an experience nothing short of tragic to make a young man understand that life is one, that act and consequence can by no means be dissevered, and a man's deeds are his destiny. This experience of law is the discovery of life; and the youth who has learned to comprehend life's unity, and include both deed and consequence, beginning and end, in one view, can henceforth " see life steadily and see it whole."

The spiritual experience of youth in the physical period of adolescence is that of individuation, the setting apart of the self from the previous environment; in the second or mental period, it is characteristically that of illumination, the discovery of the meaning and value of activities that one has chosen for himself. This illumination brings many keen disappointments. There is much of humiliation and self-reproach in it; much also of wholesome truth and saving self-discovery. When a youth makes, all for himself, his first great failure, he begins to understand himself and the world. When a course of action that he deliberately selected leads to evil and dis-

aster, he gains a practical insight into the
construction of the moral world and into his
own moral nature as well. It is good for
youth to learn, as early as possible, its own
weaknesses and limitations. We expect
the young men of every generation to renew unceasingly the quest of the hitherto
unattainable ; but that quest is more likely
to receive a substantial reward if it abjures
at the outset the absurdly impossible ;
young men should not expect to mingle fire
and water, or to hasten God's kingdom by
leaving the paths of rectitude.

Nevertheless, the illumination of youth is
not all disillusion. Even the fallen Prodigal
was no pessimist. His self-discovery revealed not only his weakness and demerit,
but his real worth as well : he was made
for something better than a swineherd.
In the orientation of the spirit, youth finds
errors to be corrected and perversities to be
overcome ; but many of its hypotheses are
confirmed, many expectations fulfilled,
many ideals realized. This is the time
when the main outlines of knowledge and
conviction are finally established. It is the

period of college life for those who go to
college, of learning a trade or business, or
trying several, for those who do not. For
all it is a time of venture and experiment,
and normal youth is shrewd to heed its
lessons. And it issues, with nearly all, in a
well-formed notion of what one means to be
and do in life, and an established set of
ideas and principles by whose light he expects to do life's work. Just as early
adolescence shows what manner of physique
a man is to have, so this middle period
determines and reveals the mental outfit
with which he is to go through the world.

The third act in the drama of the soul's
development through the years of youth
presents the readjustment of the young
life, now distinctly individualized, to the
social whole. After the achievement of
freedom and the discovery of life's whole-
ness, there follows, in the order of nature,
a new adjustment, freely and willingly
made, of one's self to one's proper sphere.
How does the soul that has found itself find
its true sphere?

Nowhere is the parable more true to

common experience than in the nature of the Prodigal's first good resolve. He sees that he is out of place, and determines to return home. There may be homesickness in this, but there is much besides. It is the awakening of the homing instinct. A factor of the soul's life of whose existence he had not been aware is unveiled. The experience of estrangement leads to the discovery that there is that within the soul which tells a man unerringly of his true place and destiny. Youth's first free years are guided by a weather-vane that seeks a favoring breeze from any quarter of the skies; then, some day, there is disclosed to the wanderer, what he has carried all along unknowingly, life's compass, whose needle points him faithfully to the spot where he belongs.

In other words, the soul of youth comes quickly to understand that utter alienation is impossible. At the very time when the assertion of self becomes most pronounced, the sense of the social value of that self awakens. The youth not only wants to be himself; he wants to be somebody in the world. He wishes to fill a place among

men. Fleeing from the limitations of childhood, the soul may choose for a time to
dwell apart ; but seclusion is not its permanent abode—its monasticism is transient ;
out of his isolation the youth means, like
Moses or Paul, to bring forth a personality
equipped for the doing of deeds in the
world. The soul that has secured its own
rights of freedom and gone apart, soon
swings about to demand a place in the
social body ; and the social impulse becomes
the controlling motive.

All progress, we are told, is by differentiation and integration. It starts with something simple. In that simple thing, whatever it may be—the cell that contains
the germ of the plant or animal life, or
the family that contains the germ of social
and national life—divisions soon appear.
Different parts are set in opposition to
each other, and that which was one becomes several or many. The next step
in the development is the combination
of these many parts into a unity more
complex and on a higher plane than the
simple unit with which the development

began; each of the different parts now functioning as a specialized organ or factor in the common life. Thus progress always works with two hands, creating differences where there was likeness, specialized organs or occupations where none existed, with the one, and with the other combining these various distinct elements into more complex unities that do a higher work.

This law of progress has a twofold illustration in the development of the youthful soul, first in the inner experience of the soul itself, and secondly in its social relations.

At the beginning of adolescence, the youth becomes estranged not only from his parents and the environment of his childhood, but from his childish self. The self of youth sets itself over against the self of childhood. He is not what he was. There is a differentiation. He clearly recognizes the new, and is likely to despise the old. There is often a painful antagonism within the soul between the self of childhood and the self of youth. But this division is to yield to the forces that make for correlation. The self of manhood combines the essential characteristics of youth with those of earlier years. The man needs the independence and self-reliance of youth ; just as imperatively he needs the child's docility, trust in powers outside himself, and sense of participation in the life of a social whole. Self-estrangement is followed by self-adjustment to a larger sphere. Childhood and youth, with all their differences and antagonisms, are embraced in a higher unity in the mature soul. That is why every youth, and every man who tarries on life's journey at the point of youthful self-will, finds the gates of the kingdom closed against him until he turns and becomes as a little child.

In outward relations, the antisocial instincts of early adolescence lead the youth to assert his independence of social control, whether represented by his parents or by institutions like the school or Sunday-school. But this estrangement is only the first step in a new line of progress ; its complement is the reconciliation that is to follow. For in the later years of adolescence, social instincts and forces become dominant again. This is the social period, and the main thing now is the attainment, by the growing soul, of a social will. The Prodigal came to it by way of reconciliation with his father. It makes little difference who the parties or what the circumstances are, if only the independent, self-assertive will of the wandering young soul comes to reconcile itself to another will. With the majority, the new adjustment is not made by a return to childhood's home and condition; it is more often by entrance into a new home of one's own. In either case, it is the homing instinct that is at work making one seek for the place that shall be permanently his; the union of his will with that of another is as necessary to the founding of the new home as to the return to the old. The Prodigal was saved by a new love for his father. The love of a young man and a young woman brings about the same kind of adjustment between free persons, the same denial of self, the same attainment of a social will. The chief fascination of the drama of youth, for most persons, lies in the story of this readjustment, this reconciliation of an independent, self-willed creature, who has cut loose from the ties of his early home, to his place in life, with the acceptance of social obligations and new ties that bind more closely than the old—that is, the story of man's love.

But while love is the most potent socializer of errant youth, it is not the only one. Every young man who succeeds in business, every one who puts intelligence and conscience into his obligations as a citizen, must attain, in some degree, the social will. It may be attained also through the simple acceptance of duty, wherever duty lies. If one has rebelled against his obligations, sought to find an easier pathway of life, been fretful and discontented because of his lot, blamed God and hated man because he could not have his own way in the world; when he returns to duty, accepts his lot, determines to make the best of it and get what satisfaction he can out of filling conscientiously the place assigned him, he attains that indispensable social will that marks the real maturity of the soul. Religion also, with its lofty altruism, its " Thou shalt love

thy neighbor as thyself," and its call to sacrifice, makes its distinctive and powerful
appeal to the social instincts of the soul.   In
this social period of youth, if nowhere else,
religion and nature work in the same direction and for the same end.   And when Love,
Duty and Religion unite to do a work
which nature herself is striving to perform,
the youth must have wandered far indeed
if that threefold cord is not strong enough
to bring him to his home.

If, then, the meaning of the action that
takes place within the soul of youth is to be
stated in general terms and comprehended
in a sentence, it is this: No man can be a
full-grown man, filling a man's place in a
family, in society, the state, or the kingdom
of God, until he knows himself as a distinct
individuality, a free person choosing his own
ways for himself by the light of his own
knowledge and experience; but neither is a
man full-grown while he stands alone in isolated self-will; only as he reconciles himself
to his place, his will to the family will, the
social will, the will of the state, the will of

God, and freely chooses for himself the
things that these wills declare to be best for
him,—only so can his soul reach full maturity.

Because the inner movement of the spirit
in its development turns upon itself in this
manner, finding its completion in the social
whole from which it set out, it is a genuine
dramatic action. But to forbid or hinder
this action at any point of its progress before it is complete is to turn the drama of
youth into a farce, or worse. Much of the
sorrow of the world seems to come from
the fact that children grow away from
parents, home and friends; the empty bird's
nest from which the little birds have flown
must do service to the sentiment of every
generation. But the sorrow is not because
of the growth; to be the father or mother
of strong men is no cause for grief. It is
the arrested development of souls that fills
the world with anguish. There are some
men who never outgrow their childhood;
never develop wills of their own beyond
the point of insisting on childish whims;
always have to depend upon the stronger

and wiser will of a brother or wife or friend to decide all important concerns for them. And there are many—it is the sorest grief on earth that there are so many—who stop growing at the point of youth's estrangement. They cut loose from parents and home, from social standards and ideals, and go through life in stubborn self-will. These are the cases that are sad; for only in such can the power of sin have its perfect work. They are the unnatural, abnormal ones; it is clean against nature to stop *there*; reprehensible, too, for they cut their spiritual development short by their own choice. The soul that knows estrangement should never be allowed to rest until it knows reconciliation also. Let the action be complete. God never meant a man to spend his life in lonely alienation from his kind and from Himself. Christ did not leave the Prodigal in the far country.

CHAPTER III

The Genesis of Christian Character

YOUTH gets its fascinating interest and its critical significance from this dramatic action in the soul that we have been reviewing. This action is, as we have seen, the inner action by which a soul achieves its true station and degree. Its theme is the transformation of the child, who is a dependent, subordinate being, into a man, who is an independent, coordinate being. First, to make the child an individual, to take his included, dependent life out of the family unity and make him a separately effective personality; then to re-socialize him on a higher plane, to embrace his individuality in the larger coordination of society,—that is the aim, and the course, of the dramatic action within the soul of youth.

In the course of this action, the youth is brought face to face with nearly all the critical questions that affect human well-be-

ing.   Every personal problem from those of
health and strength to those of ideals and
pursuits, must be met ; so must all the questions of social relations from that of obedience to parents to those of citizenship, marriage and religion.   These questions overlap
and interblend so that no one of them ever
stands wholly by itself or is settled alone ;
nor is the discussion of one of them likely
to be very profitable unless the presence
and influence of the others be recognized.
In the following discussions, the focus of attention is the religious problem, treated not
as a thing by itself but as an element in the
normal experience of youth.

The religious problem appears to the
youth in myriad forms, but is always the
same in essence.   The youth must somehow
settle his relations with the higher law, the
moral order, the spiritual and unseen world;
in a word, with God.   Some settlement
of this question every youth must make.
We of course regard the Christian solution of the religious problem as the
only satisfactory one.   We shall see that
religious experience cannot possibly mean

the same thing for all; but the only religious ideal that we find tolerable is
that of Christian discipleship, the settlement
of one's higher relationships on the Christian
plan.   The religious problem of youth, then,
in our view, becomes the problem of finding
a way for the youth into the Christian life,
of winning a Christian faith and character.

The Christian character which we desire
to see our youth attain is everywhere recognized as the efflorescence of a Christian
spirit, the manifestation of an inner life.
The question of the ways and means of at-
taining a Christian character is therefore at
bottom the question of the beginning of the
Christian life in the soul.   This beginning
is itself everywhere regarded as in some
sense a work of the Holy Spirit, the impartation to a human being of a spiritual life
that draws from the boundless deep of
Deity.   But under what circumstances does
the Spirit most commonly perform this
work?   Through what outward means or
agencies is that quality of spiritual life
which produces Christian character imparted to the soul of man?

The prevailing ideas on this subject are to be traced to four principal sources. We may pass over the first three with brief mention; but the fourth is so related to the development of youth as to demand more special attention.

The first in order is the sacramental system of the Catholic churches. According to this view, the renewing Spirit is associated with the water of baptism, and regeneration is wrought by a sacramental grace bestowed in this rite. What is needful to insure the inception of a Christian life is that one shall be placed, by birth or otherwise, within the circle of the sacramental influences that commence with baptism; within that circle, which is of course identified with the visible Church, and there alone, there is renewal and salvation for all. It is to be expected that the life imparted to the soul in baptism will be from the first the determinative factor in the formation of character; but it is to be made intelligent, given a consciousness of itself, taught to understand its own nature and aims, through the knowledge of the truth conveyed by

catechetical instruction ; and it is to become
the certain and permanent possession of the
soul only by confirmation, and to be developed to full formative power by the
sacrament of communion. This view of the
beginning of the Christian life within the
soul is manifestly a formal and institutional
view. In accordance with the claims of the
ecclesiastical system within which it was developed, it makes the reception of the new
life conditional on connection with the outward institution of religion, the Church.
Those who reject it and wonder at its continued power in the world are to remember
that the Lord's arm is not shortened that
he cannot save by means of forms and institutions as well as without them ; though not
dependent upon them, he is surely free to
use them ; and whether, or to what extent,
he does make use of them for the generation
of Christian character in human souls, is not
a question of doctrine to be decided by
argument, but a question of fact to be settled by observation.

From this conception of the genesis of the
Christian life the Reformed churches did not

at first break away; but a radical modification of it was introduced by a simple change of emphasis. Without explicitly denying the efficacy of sacramental grace bestowed in baptism, they placed more emphasis upon the truth, as summed up in the creed and catechism, as the means whereby the Spirit lays the foundation of a Christian character. If the Reformation be regarded, as it surely may be, as a part of the great intellectual awakening known as the Renaissance, it will appear that nothing could be more natural than this increased emphasis on the power of divine truth to save the soul. This was the common inspiration of the reformers. The Greek Testament of Erasmus, the German Bible of Luther, and all the great series of confessions and catechisms that culminated in those of the Westminster Assembly, point to this emphasis among Protestants on the truth as the chief means for the Spirit's renewal of the soul. The practical outcome of this view is to reduce dependence on religious institutions to the minimum; the best that human agencies can accomplish toward the impartation of the Christian life is to get the truth into the mind of the growing child or the unconverted man, trusting the Spirit to work within him and sanctify him by the truth.

In the eighteenth century, there came a complete departure from this entire mode of conceiving the Spirit's work. Another theory of the Spirit's operation, requiring correspondingly different methods in religious work, was brought forward by the Great Awakening of 1740. By this theory regeneration was conceived as consisting essentially in a change of one's tastes or sentiments. It was defined as the communication of a new spiritual sense or taste, or as "a change in the balance of the sensibilities." That a marked change in taste and sentiment accompanies the experience of adult conversion is beyond question ; if this change is itself the essential element of regeneration, then it would seem that appeals to the sentiments, affections or emotions would be more likely to promote the beginning of the Christian life than any other means. On this doctrinal presumption the methods of the great revival were developed. The psychology of that day made no distinction between the will and the sensibilities, and so the distinctive method of the revival system became an appeal to the will that was emotional in character. It was held that the beginning of the Christian life in the soul was normally attended by a great awakening of the feelings, was perhaps dependent on such an awakening, and that regeneration must be manifested by a radical change of inclination or disposition. A conscious experience of this kind became the only acceptable evidence of regeneration, and without regeneration, thus attested, men were not considered fit for membership in the church.

And so the Christian life was expected to begin, not in the silent use of the truth by the Spirit, but in circumstances that would stir the religious feelings to their depths. These circumstances were provided by the revival meeting, which was an institution expressly designed to produce such a disturbance of the customary complacent equilibrium of the soul that the desired change in the balance of the sensibilities

might easily come about. The revival
methods that began with the Wesleys,
Whitefield and Edwards were continued
after their death with undiminished popularity. The approved way of becoming a
Christian was to be converted in a protracted meeting. Attention was fixed upon
a certain type of mental agitation as the
proper evidence of the Spirit's work; in-
sistence on an experience of this kind made
it easy to undervalue early instruction in
the Christian faith and morals; the older
catechetical system died out; the Wesleyan
movement broke away from the confirmation system of the historic churches; infant
baptism was neglected, and the bodies that
reject it altogether increased with great
rapidity; institutional claims were belittled,
and the personal contact of every individual
soul with Deity in the Spirit was magnified;
and incidentally, no place was left for a
child in the Church of God, because the
Christian life was held to begin in emotions that have no place in the soul of a
child.

It was in reaction against the extreme in-

dividualism of this system that the modern
doctrine of the genesis of Christian character by nurture first appeared. The logic
of the situation demanded a powerful re-
assertion of the corporate, organic elements
of the religious life. This was made by
Horace Bushnell in his epoch-making book
entitled "Christian Nurture." The doctrine
of this book, although set forth in terms of
thought belonging to the era before the rise
of evolutionary theories, fits in so aptly
with the newer ways of thinking that it has
been generally accepted wherever the evolutionary philosophy has gone. Its agreement
with the general tendency of the last half-
century to look for vital rather than mechanical processes, and to believe that things
come to be what they are by growth rather
than by manufacture, has made it very popular. The former view, along with the revival system founded upon it, has suffered a
corresponding loss of popularity; so that
among the churches that reject the sacramentarian theory, the common expectation
of our time seems to be that the Christian
life shall begin in some kind of process of

Christian nurture. The doctrine and methods of Christian nurture must therefore be somewhat carefully examined.

To the popular mind the doctrine of Christian nurture is adequately represented by the watchword, "Growth, not conversion." Christian nurture is understood to be that method of ordering religious activities which looks for men to be made Christians by a process of growth rather than by a crisis of conversion. But that watchword involves a serious confusion of thought. It is the same confusion that has beset the evolutionary doctrines all along—the persistent notion that the discovery of the successive steps by which a thing has reached its present state makes it unnecessary to account for its origin. When the higher forms of life were found to have developed from lower, and these from lower still, there were those who thought that the question of the origin of life had been disposed of; it had not, in truth, been touched. Neither has the question of the origin of the Christian life in the soul been touched when it is seen that a Christian character is normally attained by a slow process of growth rather than by a sudden revolution in conversion.

To get rid of this confusion, we must remember that Christian nurture is a particular method of dealing with growing souls which is based on a particular theory of the genesis of the Christian life within the soul. The theory governs the method. The primary question for Christian nurture is not, as so many seem to think, as to the most successful ways of feeding and guiding the soul's growth ; the first question is as to how that particular kind of spiritual life that produces Christian character is to get into the soul. In the discussions of this subject, it seems frequently to be forgotten that life must originate before it can grow. The assumption appears to be that if a child is subjected to a properly devised course of religious instruction and training, the particular quality of spiritual life necessary to the production of Christian character can be trusted to slip in unawares at some point or other, or be produced by spontaneous generation !

Let us not mistake the real point. To

take Bushnell's thesis "that the child is to
grow up a Christian, and never know himself as being otherwise," as a statement of
the doctrine of Christian nurture is super-
ficial in the extreme.   That thesis is only the
application of a doctrine wrought out by him
with the most elaborate care.   The doctrine
itself develops a new conception of the manner of the Spirit's entrance into the soul to
kindle the divine life there.   It is founded
on the fact that there is a kind of organic
connection in character between parents and
children.   Moral and spiritual qualities are,
in a measure, transmitted by heredity ; but,
still more effectively, the workings of the
family life in its essential unity of temper,
spirit, atmosphere, ideals and purposes, tend
to reproduce the moral and spiritual likeness of the parents in their children.   The
family is an institution of such a nature that
by processes analogous to those of organic
growth, without conscious design on the
part of the parents, it will form the character of the child for good or evil.   Because
of hereditary influences, and because the
family is the supreme environment of the

child during its most plastic years, an environment, too, that works with unparalleled efficacy to mold the infant character to its own standards, it is to be expected that the spirit and character of the child will be determined, almost infallibly, by those of the family.

Therefore it is to be expected that the growing soul of the child who springs from Christian stock and unfolds his life in a Christian atmosphere will exhibit from the first, and more and more distinctly as the years advance, the Christian character, passing from a Christian childhood to a Christian youth, and on to a Christian manhood by a natural development. And the reason for this expectation is not that the divine life will slip in unawares at some stage of the soul's growth, but that it is inconceivable that the wise God should fail to make use of an agency so effective as this vital connection of child and parent to further the work of redemption. The power of this connection in transmitting the taint of sin from generation to generation has been long recognized; it is little short of blasphemy to suppose that God will allow it to work only for the propagation of sin. "The only supposition which honors God," says Bushnell, "is that the organic unity of which I speak was ordained originally for the nurture of holy virtue in the beginning of the soul's history, and that Christianity or redemption must of necessity take possession of the abused vehicle and sanctify it for its own merciful uses." There is nothing mechanical or compulsory about it. Christian character does not follow necessarily from being born to a place in a Christian family; not every child of Christian parents will become a Christian by the process of nurture. But this is to be the general expectation. The presumption is that the Spirit of God will work along the lines of vital connection to reproduce in the children the Christian character of their parents, with as much of fidelity and certitude as, by the same vital connection, their mental and physical characteristics are made to reappear.

Previous theories of the genesis of the Christian life had ignored this vital connection. But it is evident, on reflection, that

the most natural line of approach for the
Spirit of God to the soul of a child in a
Christian home is through those bonds of
connection that lie deeper than consciousness and bind life to life in the hidden mystery of being. The testimony of observation is that God does not, as a rule, bring
the child of Christian parents to himself
either by means of the truth taught in the
catechism or by a miracle of grace in conversion, but by a vital process in which the
moral and religious qualities of that circle
in which the child originates are assimilated
into his character. The Spirit finds his way
into the soul of such a one, not, most naturally, through the instructed mind, or the
aroused emotions, or new resolutions of the
will; the Spirit is life, and moves along
those deeper, stronger lines of connection
which are not always present to the consciousness through intelligence and feeling,
but are always present to the soul as essential and vital.

And so, while the sacramentarian theory
traces the genesis of Christian character to
the Spirit's use of the rite of baptism, and

the Reformed theory to the Spirit's use of the truth, and the evangelical theory to the Spirit's use of an emotional awakening, the theory of Christian nurture traces it to the Spirit's use of the necessary, vital relationship of child and parents. It looks for the child's Christian life to originate in the hidden, vital connection of his spirit with the spirit of a household that is leavened by the presence of Christ. Christ, being the spirit and atmosphere of the home, will pass into the soul of the child along those lines of necessary spiritual relationship by which all other family traits are imparted. Christian nurture may expect much from correct instruction and wise training ; but Christian nurture is not instruction or training ; it is the impartation and development of life in ways concordant with life's lofty power and fathomless mystery. And the highest life can be thus imparted because the grace of God is pledged to make use of the organic relations of human spirits for purposes of redemption.

This conception of the theory of Christian nurture reveals at once its power and its limitations as a method. Because it works by vital means and at the very fount of life, it can do almost everything for the child. But because it can do its work only through the vital ties that bind child to parent, it is rigidly limited to the home circle. It has no other possible sphere. The prerequisites of Christian nurture are a Christian parentage for the child and a Christian household in which he shall pass his early, plastic years. There are no methods of Christian nurture, but only one method,—that of the wholesome, earnest, devout family life, enveloping the child from his earliest days; "the loveliness of a good life, the repose of faith, the confidence of righteous expectation, the sacred and cheerful liberty of the Spirit—all glowing about the young soul as a warm and genial nurture, and forming in it, by methods that are silent and imperceptible, a spirit of duty and religious obedience to God."

Aside from heredity, the formative influences of the parental life upon the child are of two classes: those exercised consciously, with express design to benefit the child, and those exercised unconsciously, without thought of their effect upon him. It needs but little thought to show that of these two sets of influences the second is vastly the more important. Lessons, counsel, training, correction, given with the intent of guiding the child into the right way are all important, but not so important as the atmosphere of the home life. In the ordering of the household, the conduct of family affairs, the temper habitually displayed, the language commonly used, the sincerity and openness or the deception and distrust of the parents toward each other, the genuineness and simplicity of their religious faith or its formality and factitiousness,—in these and a thousand similar things the real character and spirit of the parents is shown without reserve, and is undesignedly but indelibly impressed upon their children. Christian parents ought to make it their deliberate design to lead their children to Christ ; but their designs should always keep the fact in view that the influence that they unconsciously wield is sure to have more effect upon the children's

characters than any of their conscious
efforts to do them good. It all comes
back at last to what the parents are.

Consequently there can be no possible
method devised for supplying Christian
nurture to those whose parents and homes
are not genuinely Christian in spirit and
character. The conditions on which Christian nurture depends for the inception of
the Christian life in the soul are wholly
wanting with these. Nothing can take the
place of daily Christian living in the home,
or do what the home fails to do. There is
no substitute for a Christian father and
mother. Others may give the children
some of their instruction and inspiration,
their training and education; but others
can give them Christian nurture only as
they would give them bodily nurture, by
taking them entirely away from the un-
faithful parents and placing them in a truly
Christian home. They are much deluded
who imagine that the development of the
organized forms of institutional religious
life can make good the lack of Christian
homes. Christian nurture is no function of

the church; it is not an affair of Sunday-schools, Young People's Societies, cate-chetical classes, or anything of that kind. A church or Sunday-school cannot give nur-ture; for the same reason that a Home can-not be a home.[1] The Church must do its best to bring those of unchristian antece-dents and surroundings into the Christian life; but the one thing which it cannot give them, the one method on which it must not count, is Christian nurture.

Another limitation of Christian nurture, in which we are soon to see a great signifi-cance, is that its chief work must be done at the beginning of the child's life. It has been remarked that one of Bushnell's most remarkable anticipations of the scientific conclusions of our own time is this: "The most important age for Christian nurture is the first. . . . More, as a general fact, is done, or lost by neglect of doing, on a child's immortality, in the first three years

[1] In "Timothy's Quest," Mrs. Kate Douglas Wiggin shows what a difference the capital letter makes to a child. "He was very clear on one point, and that was that he would never be taken alive and put in a Home with a capital H."   Page 172.

of his life, than in all his years of discipline afterwards."

Our present interest in this limitation is not in the important rules for dealing with young children that are to be deduced from it, but rather in the suggestion which it gives concerning the relation of Christian nurture to the religious problem as it presents itself to youth. That the child's earliest years are its most plastic, that it is most sensitive and responsive to the formative influence of the parental life in the days when it is utterly dependent, that with the growth of bodily strength and the power of thought and expression the child begins to lose plasticity though still remaining in the matrix of the home life, are facts of the greatest import for those who would bring their young children up in the nurture and admonition of the Lord. Our special concern, however, is to see what becomes of Christian nurture when the disturbances of youth break out. This will be the theme of the next chapter to which the present is linked by this consideration :—*Because Christian nurture works by the vital connection of parent and child, it must get its work done before the individuation of the child takes place ; and because that individuation must, in the nature of things, take place, Christian nurture is to be regarded as intrinsically a preparatory, never a final, work.*

CHAPTER IV

Where Christian Nurture Fails

EFFECTIVE and well-nigh omnipotent as Christian nurture appears to be with childhood, with the dawn of youth its power begins suddenly, strangely, but certainly, to wane. When we look that it should bring forth grapes, it often brings forth wild grapes, or even only the ashes of disappointment.

One would expect that the children who have had the advantages of Christian nurture would, on reaching adolescence, manifest a decided superiority over those without such advantages in dealing with the religious problem. But the facts in this connection are distinctly disappointing. Of course the old saw about ministers' sons and deacons' daughters has only a grain of truth in it; but that grain is significant. It does often happen that those who have been most carefully and lovingly nurtured exhibit pronounced irreligious tendencies in youth, while those who have been without religious influences at home often become most earnest and acceptable Christians.

One way of explaining this is to say that Christian parents do not always know how to deal with their children, and that their nurture is consequently faulty—which is likely to be and remain true as long as parents are mortal and fallible; while on the other hand, there are few families, even the most openly irreligious, whose children are not disciplined in some of the fundamental requirements of that law of morals which is a schoolmaster to lead men to Christ. This explanation is quite true, but wholly insufficient. It ignores the deeper cause that we are trying to get recognized, namely, the work that nature is doing in the soul of the youth himself.

The real reason why so many children of Christian nurture become irreligious youths, while children without such nurture manifest a deeply religious spirit at adolescence, is found in the self-estrangement of the youthful soul. This is nature's way of evening up the religious opportunities and responsibilities of the two classes. She makes the child of the Christian home take the attitude of a stranger toward his early training, the standards and ideals in which he has been nurtured, and the habits already formed, in order that he may learn whether these things are really a part of him or not; he must find himself at any cost, and if his true self be not in these things, he must know it. This makes him, at least for a time and in a measure, appear irreligious. On the other hand, nature makes the child of the irreligious home feel himself a stranger to the ideals and practices of that circle, takes him into that region of religious faith and aspiration which is to him the far country, and asks him to find himself there. And so it comes about that the advantage of the one and the handicap of the other are very nearly canceled, and the children of Christian and unchristian homes approach the questions of religion in youth with minds alike open to the truth, and with far less of favorable or unfavorable

predisposition than we should expect. The
real advantage of the child of Christian
parents lies, not in having religious questions already decided when he reaches
adolescence, but, as we shall see later, in a
very different direction.

In our interpretation of the inner drama
of youth, we have used the parable of the
Prodigal Son to illustrate a certain estrangement of soul, in order to a realization of
individual freedom and responsibility, which
was set forth as a natural, normal element
in the spiritual experience of adolescence.
Lest it should be thought that it is natural
only to prodigals, and that it is dangerous
to admit that such a feeling has any rightful place in the soul, we must take further
pains to show its true character and its
practical necessity. For contrast with the
prodigal we take, not his older brother, nor
any ordinary boy ; we take the boy Jesus himself. The universal truth of estrangement
and reconciliation has its illustration in the
experience of the universal man.

The full meaning of our Lord's story of
the boy that was lost and found again,

dawns first upon us when we connect it with
the fact that our Lord himself, in the early
days of his youth, was lost and found
again.

Just one incident of the youth of Jesus is
recorded in the sacred volume; and that is
the story of his break with his parents, and
his reconciliation to them.   How illumi-
nating this record is! and how enhearten-
ing!   Lest we should think that because our
youthful estrangement always does involve
sin it always must, and the thought depress
us beyond measure, the archetypal man
passed through it, was lost and found again,
without sin.

" After three days they found him in the
temple."   The words recall the whole story
—no need to repeat it.   Only observe that
this was the meaning of youth to Jesus—
separation from his parents and entrance
into a larger sphere.   No longer did the
word of father and mother suffice him: he
must inquire of the doctors in the temple!
Nay, not even they could satisfy his adolescent mind; he listened to them with respect, but questioned their conventional re-

plies ; and they were amazed at the penetration and independence of thought displayed
in his words.   Thus the soul of Jesus, like
the soul of every other boy, began on entering youth to round itself off into a separate
individuality.   That first separation from
his parents was the significant beginning of
an estrangement of soul that made Jesus
more and more to stand alone until he became the one Perfect Individual, the realized
ideal of manhood, hailed everywhere with
mocking words now made worshipful, " Behold, the man ! "

   But the priceless comfort of this record is
that while Jesus was growing up beyond his
parents, he was not growing away from
them.   He could exceed them without an-
tagonizing them ; as the luxuriant vine that
covers a whole trellis never despises the little narrow space of earth through which it
came forth into the free air and sunshine.
The first independent act of our Lord that
is recorded was this : " The boy Jesus tar-
ried behind in Jerusalem."   For that act he
felt no contrition when his parents found
him ; his only words were of surprise that

they should not have known that he would
be in his Father's house. He was not sorry
that he had lingered ; he did not repent of
having sought instruction that his parents
were not competent to give. But this first
assertion of his independent selfhood involved no stubborn self-will ; as there was
no sin to repent of, so there was no obstacle
to make reconciliation difficult. " He went
down with them, and came to Nazareth ;
and he was subject unto them."

Years afterward there came a day when
Jesus declared his independence of his
mother in more explicit words, that have
always seemed harsh to us : " Woman, what
have I to do with thee ? " Nevertheless, he
found it possible even then to reconcile himself to her wish and do what she desired.
Still later, when men said, " He is beside
himself," and his relatives came to lead him
away, he declared his independence of them
only to assert his union with mankind :
" Who is my mother and my brethren ?
And looking round on them that sat round
about him, he saith, Behold, my mother and
my brethren ! For whosoever shall do the

will of God, the same is my brother, and sister, and mother." So, step by step, throughout his whole life, Jesus linked each self-assertion of his individual soul to an act in which he identified himself with a higher will. Never on earth was elsewhere seen such self-assertion as that of Jesus, passing up from the confident words of a teacher to his pupils to culminate in the astounding declaration, " All authority hath been given unto me in heaven and on earth." Yet never did earth see such humility, for this soul, so remarkably individualized, seemed never to be separate from the Highest. " I can of myself do nothing. . . . I seek not mine own will, but the will of him that sent me."

And if any one imagines that this perfect reconciliation with the Father's will required no effort on the part of Jesus, that he never found himself in a far country whence he could return to his Father only at great cost, let him remember Gethsemane, and judge by the struggling of that soul that was exceeding sorrowful even unto death, and by that agonizing prayer, and by that bloody sweat, how much it cost the Saviour to achieve his final reconciliation with his Father and the lot appointed him, so that he could say, " Not my will, but thine, be done! "

We find, then, two distinct types of the estrangement of youth. The Prodigal sinned; Jesus did not. The one represents self-discovery through an experience involving some moral offense; the other shows that it is possible to attain individual and social perfection without sin. We are led therefore to expect marked differences in the experience of youth at the period of adolescent estrangement. Some will approach the type of the Prodigal; others, though not without sin, will approach the type presented in Jesus.

It has been common to treat the difference as wholly a moral difference : the boys of the one type are called bad boys, the others good. · Or it has been said, when a youth went the way of the Prodigal, that there must have been something wrong with his home training, and a wiser Christian nurture might have prevented his fall. In reality the difference is largely temperamental. It appears among children of the best

Christian homes as certainly as elsewhere. Before we conclude that Christian nurture can make Christian men and women of our children without any imitation of the Prodigal by any of them, we must patiently consider the effect of temperament upon the religious experience of youth.

Even those who have least use for physiological psychology recognize the correlation of the spiritual nature with the brain and nervous system. The two sets of nerves, sensor and motor, correspond to two sides of the spiritual nature, the receptive and the active. In every individual, one side of the nervous system, and the corresponding side of the spiritual nature, tends to predominate. Some are more active, others more receptive. Some are quick, energetic, practical; others are slow, thoughtful, sentimental. The first are called quick-tempered; the second, easy or even-tempered. This is the primary distinction between the tempers or temperaments of men. It is crossed by another line of distinction dividing the strong from the weak, or, more accurately, the intense from the moderate. This gives

four great types of temperament, corresponding rather closely with the four tradi-
tional types. There is the weak motor
temperament, that of the enthusiast, called
the sanguine. The strong motor temperament is that of the men of action, the intense, hot-tempered men; it was formerly
called the choleric, but the ancient name is
without significance now, and a more de-
scriptive term is desirable, such as "energetic." The strong sensor temperament is
that of the man of thought, reflection and
sentiment; some have replaced the ancient
meaningless name "melancholic" by "sentimental"; we prefer "reflective" as more
accurate. Finally, the weak sensor temperament is that of the slow-and-steady man,
the sluggish man, or the heavy conserva-
tive; it is called the "phlegmatic," and the
word has passed into common speech with
just the meaning attached to it here.

Few mature people exhibit the characteristics of any one of these temperaments in
their purity, because the work of education
does so much to bring one's nature into balance, overcoming the excesses of one's pe-

culiar temperament. But at the time of adolescence, temperamental peculiarities assert themselves with full vigor; and they are strong enough to determine the form, and often to affect the content, of the youth's religious experience.

What, then, is the influence of temperament upon religion? It has been observed that there is a predominance of persons of the sanguine and reflective temperaments in the churches, especially in those circles within the churches that are counted more spiritual. It has also been observed that the spiritual exercises of the Church, in both Catholic and Protestant communions, appeal especially to these two temperaments; the Catholic ideal of spirituality finds response chiefly among the reflective or sentimental, while the preaching, songs and methods of the Protestant revival, or the " wide-awake " prayer-meeting, are especially adapted to the sanguine. From these facts it is easy to infer that the predominance of sanguine and reflective people in the Church is due to the fact that its exercises appeal especially to these two temperaments, and that a

change in the character of these exercises
would bring in a predominance of the energetic or phlegmatic men. But it would be
just as true to say that the exercises of the
church suit these temperaments best because
there has always been a majority of this
class of people in the church to determine
what the tone of the church life should be.
The real reason for the predominance of the
sanguine and reflective temperaments among
the more actively religious people lies in a
different direction.

It is the exceedingly simple reason, that
religion is easier for these temperaments
than for the others.

Reduced to the simplest possible terms—
or term—religion is love. The love that is
religion, whether shown toward God or fel-
low man, is essentially a self-devotion.
What religion requires of every man is that
he shall subdue himself in unselfish love.
This involves a fundamental self-surrender
to a higher will, a conscious self-subjection
to the law of a Master, an enlistment in his
cause. This is not easy for any, perhaps, but
it is easier for two types of men than for two

others. Your sanguine man will find it comparatively easy; if only his enthusiasm is stirred, it will carry him on. Your reflective man will find it not so hard, because his sober convictions and dearest sentiments point that way. But your active, energetic, hot-tempered man, the forceful man that does most of the rough-and-ready work of the world, will find it exceedingly hard, because the self in him is far more intensely assertive, and cannot be so readily subdued. And your slow, phlegmatic man will find it hard, because the appeal for self-devotion awakens no enthusiasm, kindles no responsive fires, in his breast; religion for him must be a matter of cool calculation and clear perception of duty. Here is the constitutional reason for the predominance of the sanguine and reflective temperaments in the Church; it is because these temperaments find self-conquest, self-devotion to another's cause, self-surrender to a higher will, much easier than the others.

But the value of an attainment is measured by its difficulty. The men who become Christians hardest often make the best

Christians. Religion does its greatest work in those temperaments that respond to it least readily. Nathanael was a reflective temperament, an Israelite in whom there was no guile before he ever met with Jesus; but even after becoming one of the chosen Twelve he never did a single thing significant enough to be recorded. Peter was a great, robust, hot-tempered, coarse-grained, profane man, with a lot of work for grace to do in his nature before he could be sanctified; but Peter was worth more to the cause of Christ than a hundred Nathanaels. It has probably always been true, and is likely to be true in the future, that the sanguine and reflective temperaments form the majority among professed Christians; but the minority, made up of forceful men of action and those slow and steady natures that can hold on and endure with inexhaustible patience, do the most effective work and wield the greatest influence. The sanguine temperament gives us the most enthusiastic leaders, the most stirring preachers, the most affecting singers; the reflective temperament furnishes most of the scholars and thinkers; but the energetic and phlegmatic temperaments supply the most effective organizers and administrators, the best missionaries, and the most reliable supporters of the Church.

This consideration of temperamental differences furnishes a most suggestive insight into the behavior of young people when the estrangement of youth comes over them. The sanguine boy is very likely to be "carried away" with something; if with enthusiasm for religion—usually represented to him by some class or society—it is well, only we are to remember that he may be one of those who, having no root in themselves, soon wither. The reflective boy will be the doubter, astonish you with skeptical questions, and have real and serious struggles with his beliefs and convictions; he will do the most earnest thinking, and be most likely to come into the church from the Sunday-school or pastor's class. The active, energetic boy, who always plunges deep when he goes in at all, is very likely to be the prodigal, and the sluggish, phlegmatic boy will be the tame elder brother, who never goes into the far country and never learns the depth and sweetness of the Paternal love in whose sunshine he daily moves. In general, it is pretty sure that the boys of sanguine and energetic temperaments—the " motor-minded " youth, will experience a more violent estrangement, go further in risks of sin, break more completely with their past training and ideals, than the others. There is therefore a deep reason in human nature why some boys should follow in youth the example of the Prodigal, and some the example of Jesus ; and that reason is not that those of the one class are worse morally than the others, but that they are different temperamentally. Whence it follows, that no system of Christian nurture or culture can possibly secure anything like a uniform religious experience for those of different temperaments. Only dismal disappointment waits for him who expects to bring these four boys to Christ in the same way.

There is another matter to be considered here. Sex, as well as temperament, has much to do with the form that religious ex-

perience takes in youth. For one thing, it
is pretty well established that women, by
nature, approach more nearly on the whole
to the sanguine and reflective types of temperament among men than to the others;
not that there are no energetic or phlegmatic women, but that their energy is not so
coarse, and their passivity seldom so dull.
Therefore, the same reasons that make the
sanguine and reflective types of men prevail
in the church, tend to bring in a majority
of women. The women are most likely to
respond to appeals that are suited to men of
those types. Moreover, the requirement of
self-devotion finds in the feminine nature its
preeminent object. The kind of self-devotion that religion requires comes far more
easily to women than to even sanguine or
reflective men. It is easier by nature, and
long custom has made it easier still. Self-
devotion, self-surrender to another, self-con-
secration to another's cause, have always
been woman's peculiar privilege, her most
winsome characteristic, and her most commanding claim on man's grateful love. A
deep instinct of humanity says that it is

good and right that a woman should give herself to her husband, leaving home, family, friends, even her very name, to identify herself with him and his. And it is clean against nature to reverse the process, simply because nature has made it easier for women to surrender their all in self-devotion than for men.

That is one reason why religion, in its essence, comes easier to women than to men. There is another, which applies with especial force to the organized and social religion of the church. It is because women are more racial by constitution than men. Here is surely one of the deepest differences between the sexes. There is a certain great racial type of what nature means a human being to be, maintained from age to age. Scientists have observed that in the course of evolution, it is through the female that this type is maintained. The male is not so constant; he is more completely, sometimes extravagantly, individualized; in him the most pronounced variations appear; nature tries her boldest experiments with him. It is natural to expect in man, therefore, the more pronounced and extreme individualities, while woman keeps closer to the racial type. He goes forth to seek new good, while she conserves and passes on to future generations the good already attained by the race. This means that in religion man's nature impels him to seek a new and unique religious experience for himself, while woman's moves her to take up and hold fast the approved good in the experience of the race. She is therefore more social in her religious experience, goes more easily with a company, conforms without serious objection to custom and convention in this as in other things; while man is more individual, fights out more battles with sin and doubt alone, rebels more often against conventional ideas and practices, and compasses a wider sweep of wandering before he settles in his Father's house. For this reason it is more natural for women than for men to join the church. We do not say, or believe, that they are more religious than men; but conventional and social religion comes more easily to them. The very thing that makes it easier for the

women to follow the fashions and maintain
the social conventionalities, also makes it
easier for them to find their places in the
church. And if a church has more male
than female members, there is something
abnormal in its condition, and it is not especially to be congratulated.

But here again, religion's hardest work is
its best work. A church made up wholly of
women would not be a very influential
church. But a few strong men, who have
had manful struggles with doubt and sin,
and deep personal experiences of salvation,
when united with twice their number of
faithful women, make up a church full of
power. The constitutional difference between the sexes that we have just considered suggests that as a rule religion must
hold its own through the women ; it must
make its chief advances through the men.
The great work of preserving and passing
on to posterity the garnered good of the
ages is largely a work that men cannot do.
But the advances of each new age are made
by the incorporation into the religious body
of new and distinctive individuals, men of

pronounced character and critical experience of the religious verities that bear especially upon the present. Without the women, the Church would soon be scattered; without the men it would be fossilized.

It is now obvious that the kind of Christian nurture that suffices to bring the girls into the church, when in adolescence their racial instincts awake to life, will not suffice for the boys, because their instincts impel them to a widely different experience. Boy and girl are religious beings of different mold. It is stupid in us not to see it; and it is folly, if not sin, for us to blame the boy for yielding a less ready obedience to religious influences than his sister yields.

Is there then a normal type of religious experience for youth? Manifestly not. Differences of temperament and sex make that forever impossible. The one thing common to all youthful experiences is the realization of a separate personality, a personal character. But not all can realize a personal character, even a character copied from the divine model given in Jesus, by the same course. One method is for the youth

to enter gradually upon the new possession
of his own mind and character, taking the
lessons of childhood one by one and testing
them by the larger experience into which he
has come; finding point by point, with increasing delight, that his personal experience
of life corresponds with the teaching of his
early years and proves it true; until at last
his whole fund of knowledge, his entire religious mind, is made over into a new possession, and he is renewed in spirit through
a personal experience of growth in knowledge and grace, and finds himself firmly
grounded in the essentials of a Christian
character.

But for those of different temperament,
the achievement of individual character
means a sweeping declaration of independence of all the teaching and practices of early years. They doubt the truth
of the lessons that they have been taught,
not point by point in the way of testing
them, but all in bulk. They put themselves
in opposition to their early training and the
wisdom expressed in it. The more completely they have been enveloped in a relig-

ious atmosphere, the more deeply do they
feel the impulse to get entirely away from
it and look at life from a wholly different
standpoint. They cut loose from early associations, break off good habits already
formed, experiment with many questionable
things; lend a hospitable ear to theories of
life that deny religion and ignore morality;
find themselves in a skeptical world, seek the
reason for the skepticism, then share it;
lose, for a time at least, all sympathy with
their early Christian training, all Christian
convictions, faith and hope. Like the
Prodigal they go into the far country, and
do not seem to be able to find themselves in
any other way. When they do come to
themselves, they are amazed and pained to
see what a sinful self it is to which they
have come. Innocence has been lost, and
life is all marred with streaks of sin; bad
habits have been formed and fixed; ill has
been done, and ill deserved; henceforth
their only hope of becoming men in whom
the image of God may be seen lies in a
radical, revolutionary renewal of the spirit
of their mind. There must be a decisive

change, a transformation, a conversion from an evil life.

The point to be enforced here is that this type of experience is prescribed by human nature and provided for in the gospel as truly as the other. The expectation that Christian nurture will generally insure the attainment of Christian character without such experiences has no better ground than the former expectation that such experiences were always necessary because human nature was totally depraved. Each theory makes a specific type of human nature the exclusive one. The question whether a boy, brought up under Christian nurture, shall achieve a personal faith and character by gradual growth, testing his faith point by point until he is well assured of its validity, or by the more violent method of breaking with his past, finding new and often evil associations, trying the life of infidelity, and then coming back to his father's faith, if he ever comes at all, with a deep sense of personal sin, is very largely a question of temperament. To some extent it may be a question of his treatment in youth by his

parents and teachers; but fundamentally, it
is a question of his own nature—the nature
that God gave him and meant for his blessing, not for his loss. Certain temperaments
are more likely to enter into a Christian life
by the gradual steps of uneventful growth;
others, often the more strenuous, vigorous
ones, must have a more stormy career, a
more extreme experience, and enter the
higher life by a more marked revolution.
But both ways are right ways, both ways
are God's ways, and neither should ever be
lost sight of by the Church. So long as
there are in this world men of impulsive
natures, quick tempers, ardent, enthusiastic,
sanguine or stormy temperaments, as well
as men more sedate and evenly poised, so
long must the Church give attention to the
conversion of mature men as well as to the
nurture of children and youth.

It is evident that the estrangement, which
we have seen to be a natural and essential
feature of nature's work in the soul of youth,
is always likely to carry those of sanguine or
energetic temperaments into the far country
where the Prodigal went, in spite of all that

Christian nurture can do for them. What advantage, then, has the child of Christian nurture?

Much every way; but chiefly this, that even in the far country he still knows himself to be a child of God, and says, "My Father." The Prodigal is by no means the sorriest figure in the story. Far worse off than he is the "citizen of that country," who never had any other home or knew any better life. The life of sin is his native element; to it he was born; every one, himself included, always expected him to lead that life. Often, alas! he is perfectly content with it. If he is converted, he must break away from all that has been bred into him, from all his associations, ambitions and pursuits; he must learn the Christian ideals and ways as something wholly new, and come as a stranger into the household of the faith. The conversion of the Prodigal is also a turning from evil to righteous ways; but it is a turning back to ways of righteousness familiar to his feet from infancy. The infinite advantage of the Prodigal over the far country native, the child of Christian nurture over the child of the street, is that at the farthest point of prodigal wandering he still knows a better life and knows it as his true place, remembers higher ideals and a sphere where they are realized by his kin, has a thousand memories and associations that unite with the pleas of his friends, the prayers and tears of his parents, to win him back to the life to which he was born and of which he is a part. Christian nurture cannot keep all the boys from a prodigal's career; but it does, again and again, make the difference between the prodigal who returns penitent and is saved and the wanderer who finds the far country to his mind and dwells there content.

Some one, pleading for the children, has said that in time past the churches well-nigh reversed the saying of the Saviour, and the children were practically told, "Except ye become as grown men, and be converted, ye cannot enter into the kingdom of heaven." In our time the pendulum of thought is swinging to the other extreme, and there is danger that, with our emphasis on Christian nurture and early entrance into the church, we are about to say, in effect, to the men, "Even if you are converted and become as little children, your habits are so fixed and your character so settled that your chance of entering the kingdom of heaven is extremely small." It will never do to forget that the Saviour who said, "Suffer the little children to come unto me, and forbid them not," and received and blessed the children two or three times in his career, made it his daily labor to call sinners to repentance, to seek and save the lost, to sit at meat with publicans and sinners and offer them all the treasures of his kingdom. Only by deserting the methods of the Master can we give the conversion of mature men, yes, of hardened sinners, a secondary place in our expectations and our Christian efforts.

Blessed are those souls that find their God by the smooth path of unconscious Christian growth, with no weary wandering in the ways of flagrant sin. Blessed are those who settle their personal relations with God in the happy days of youth, starting right

in life, or discovering a wrong start quickly
and hastening back to Christ. But when
youth has passed without a Christian experience that leads to confession, let no man
think that his day of grace is past. For all
the greater experiences of life, which the
Creator has appointed for his children, are
designed to win them away from sin and the
love of sin, to renew the spirit of their
minds with a deep sense of their need of
divine friendship and fellowship; and if the
spirit of a man is not set right with God in
youth, as indeed it ought to be, then the
heavenly Father has wisely and lovingly
ordained all these sober years of responsibility and work, all the deep experiences of
human love and sorrow, and these solemn
days of age when life's work is done, to win
men to a right and loving spirit toward himself. God nurtures his children through all
their threescore years and ten; and he
faints not, neither is weary, when his labor
seems in vain and they wander afar from
him; for he knows that when, at last, the
day of repentance shall come, that man will
love most to whom most is forgiven.

CHAPTER V

The Evangelism of Jesus

THE practical interest of the investigation of the religious mind of youth centers in the question, What means and methods of Christian work will most certainly and effectively promote the achievement of a Christian character?

In the discussion of this matter hitherto, attention has been chiefly directed to two methods of making disciples, the method of the evangelist and the method of Christian nurture. The two methods have been set in sharp contrast, and the partisans of each have vigorously and even bitterly decried the other. We have just seen, however, that there is reason for holding that both methods are grounded in permanent and characteristic movements of the spiritual life, so that both are likely to continue in use with no real abatement of power, though with considerable abatement of expectations, when the intrinsic limitations of each are fully recognized.

Serious defects are, indeed, inherent in both methods. The method of the evangelist has been subjected to severe criticism because of its extreme liability to abuse. The revival, as we have seen, is an institution meant to stir the religious feelings to their depths with a mighty appeal to hope and fear and aspiration, in order to produce such a disturbance of the usual balance of the emotions that a new adjustment of the spiritual life may easily come about; and it aims to create this disturbance in a multitude of men at once, and move them in the mass. It is inevitable that a method which thus works on all with means designed to move the hardened and awake the sluggish, should put a violent strain upon natures that need no such vigorous stirring, and often work them real and serious harm. This danger besets the method in the hands of the wisest evangelist; and the mischief wrought by the unwise is past all reckoning. Yet the purpose to reach and arouse those whom less demonstrative methods fail to touch, those mature and hardened sinners who are not amenable to the gentler leading of the ordinary means of grace, is a legitimate and laudable one; and while we hope that the day of the illiterate, self-appointed, obstreperous evangelist, with a harsh voice and a narrow experience and a limp Bible and a fund of stories and little else, is past or rapidly passing, we gladly recognize in the true evangelist of apostolic spirit a man sent from God, who ought to be no stranger in the churches.

The method of Christian nurture is also open to serious criticism. Its defect is, not that it is abused, but that it is so little used as to be wholly inadequate. In the nature of the case, it is a method applicable only to a minority of each generation. It is distinctively the method of the devout family; it requires a Christian home as its field, and a family circle richly pervaded with the spirit of Christ; its most important period is the first three years of the child's life; it works by vital forces and unconscious influences more than by deliberate intention and effort; it requires parents to be priests to bring their children to God, the home life to be the matrix to mold their souls for Christ, and family government to be the pattern of the divine order in which the child's will and conscience shall be gradually and almost unconsciously adjusted to the higher law. But as a matter of fact, the Christian homes that meet these conditions and bring forth the ripe fruit of Christian nurture are comparatively few. Family religion is more and more neglected; the family altar is a thing unknown in the majority even of Christian homes. By far the larger part of our young people are coming out of homes where the mention of personal religion is carefully avoided, and parental example is at best a divided influence; while as for Bushnell's doctrine of the out-populating power of the Christian stock, the best that can be said is that there is a certain large truth in the idea as applied to the Christian races among the peoples of the world, but no apparent truth whatever in the idea that, in our land, the avowedly Christian families will "out-populate" those where acknowledged personal religion is unknown.

And so it has come to pass that our churches have found both methods wanting, and have ceased to place their chief reliance for making disciples on either, or on the two combined. The hope of rearing children in Christian households to out-populate the unchristian families among us has vanished, if indeed it ever was seriously entertained. Yet the danger and folly of letting children grow up as sinners to be converted later on has been brought home to the conscience of the Church so strongly as to make it altogether impossible to fall back upon the revival method as completely as in former days. We have simply been forced to develop another method, making use of other means.

By common consent, the churches of the present time have consigned both the revivalistic and the Christian nurture methods of winning men to a secondary place, and committed their chief hopes to the method of educational evangelism. It is indeed a sorry fact, but it is a fact that bulks large in the planning of religious work to-day, that the church cannot trust the home to do

its part.   For this reason, there is practically
no recognition of Christian nurture in the
organization of religious work. No distinction is made between the children of Christian families and others.   They are taken
into the same classes, and given the same
instruction and discipline.   And good, earnest, sensible Christian parents, who are
trying to do their part, are content, with
seldom an objection, to have their children
taught the same lessons, touched by the
same influences, moved by the same appeals,
as the children of unchristian homes.

A colossal blunder, surely!   Nay, it is no
such thing.   The fact that children of such
different antecedents are often grouped together and given the same treatment does
not prove that Sunday-school officers and
teachers are blockheads without a ray of
intelligence in ordering their work; it
proves that common sense has recognized
in religious education, as in secular, a work
of such beneficence and such dimensions that
all children are profited by it, whatever their
antecedents.

The principle which lies at the foundation

of this new conception of evangelism is, that Christian character can be formed by education; or, in other words, that the Holy Spirit can do his transforming and sanctifying work upon the soul through educational means, no less than by conversion on the one hand, or Christian birth and growth on the other. The most favored child of Christian lineage needs the stimulus of educational contact and fellowship with those unlike himself to develop a ripened, robust, well-rounded Christian character. And on the other hand, there is a power in the truth of God, educationally applied to the growing soul, to counteract the worst possible heredity and home environment; for have we not all seen those who came out of the worst conditions, children with every human reason to be spoiled and ruined, growing up to a pure, strong, consecrated manhood and womanhood, without ever knowing an hour of true Christian nurture, nor yet any marked experience of conversion? If we can effect a real contact of the child's mind with the truth of Jesus, and, even for an hour now and then, bathe

his spirit in the spirit of Jesus, there can be
formed in him a Christian character against
which hell shall not prevail, though en-
trenched in his own home.

Much has been said and written of late
about "the new evangelism." Far and wide
Christian people are entertaining such
thoughts as these:—Revivals are no longer
popular; protracted meetings have reached
an end; the itinerant evangelist is less effective than he was—where is the Whitefield
or Finney or Moody to move the masses to-
day? The minister who trusts to occasional
awakenings for the gathering of the harvest
is voted a failure; the church so dead as to
need reviving is recreant to its work. But
while we mourn the waning of the old
evangelism, we hear the acclamations that
proclaim the rising of the new. If the old
way is dying, let it die; a new has been
born, and "God fulfills himself in many
ways, lest one good custom should corrupt
the world." The new evangelism works by
means of Sunday-schools, Young People's
Societies, catechetical classes, and pastors'
meetings with the young; it studies psychol-

ogy and pedagogy, investigates the mind
of the child, the phenomena of adolescence,
the spiritual nature of the mature man in
normal and pathological conditions ; it works
quietly, but with a purpose that is deep and
broad and long—it knows how to wait as
well as work ; it avoids excitement and display, trusting the still small voice to do
more for the salvation of souls than blatant
advertising ; it honors all the services of the
church, all the religion of the home, as
means of making disciples of Christ, and
seeks to supplement them, not by anything
extraordinary and sensational, but by healthy
and constant personal influence.   A few ac-
cessions at each communion of the church, or
a goodly class once a year, are the ideal aimed
at ; and when a church does report large
numbers added to its membership, it is
common now to add that there have been
no appeals to the emotions, no special meetings, no artificial methods, often no helpers
for the minister except the people of his own
congregation.

Perhaps such language is too explicit, for
popular thought about the new evangelism

is nebulous, and the movement itself is, like infant movements generally, vague and uncertain, with many clutches at the moon. But two things are perfectly clear to all: there is a widespread loss of confidence in the evangelistic methods of the past; and there is an insistent demand for an effective system of religious education. One who meditates with penetration on these two facts will be convinced that the new evangelism has the breath of life in it, and a great future before it.

For it will be plain to him that all true evangelism must be educational. Education is the development of the inner capacities of the soul. It is not possible, declares President Butler, of Columbia College, "for us ever again to identify education with mere acquisition of learning. . . . It must mean a gradual adjustment to the spiritual possessions of the race." But the adjustment of life to the spiritual realities with which men have to do is precisely the work of evangelism. Just as every intellectual discipline assumes and addresses the capacity of the soul for thought, so evangelism as-

sumes and addresses its capacity for God.
The evangelism that fails to meet the educational test, that merely offers men something from without and seeks to elicit nothing from within, is not adapted to the
nature of the soul that it would save or
fitted for the work that it undertakes to do.
Missionaries have always learned this by experience; and since St. Paul taught daily for
two years in the school of Tyrannus, they
have never been the ones to put asunder the
evangelistic appeal and the educational development.

It will also be plain that the new evangelism, in its effort to work out an effective educational system for winning souls to God, is
a return to the method of the Master. Jesus
was both preacher and teacher; but his
purpose was one; all his teaching was
evangelistic, all his preaching educational.
As the Church approaches the method of
Jesus in dealing with men, its evangelism
will certainly become more educational, its
efforts at religious education more profoundly evangelistic.

Consider the evangelism of Jesus.   He

proceeds upon the assumption that the kingdom of God is native to every human soul. He said, "The kingdom of God is within you." He dealt with men upon that basis. He sought, not to impart to human nature something that does not inherently belong to it, but to bring forward into clear consciousness and fruitful activity the higher potentialities of the soul. Says Browning in Paracelsus:

" Truth is within ourselves ; it takes no rise
  From outward things, whate'er you may believe.
  There is an inmost center in us all,
  Where truth abides in fulness; and around,
  Wall upon wall, the gross flesh hems it in,
  This perfect, clear perception—which is truth.
  A baffling and perverting carnal mesh
  Binds it, and makes all error : and, to KNOW,
  Rather consists in opening out a way
  Whence the imprisoned splendor may escape,
  Than in effecting entry for a light
  Supposed to be without.''

What Browning here says of truth and knowledge, we understand Jesus to say of character and salvation. The very word salvation implies the native richness and worth of the soul that is to be saved.

From our standpoint, the problem of bringing souls to God shapes itself this way : How shall the spiritual powers now dormant in the soul of the child or lying in helpless incarceration behind dense walls of worldliness and selfishness and sensuality in the mature sinner, find their way forth into light and activity ? How shall man's capacity for conformity to the will of God be set free to realize itself in action ? How shall a way be made through the grossness and sordidness of the sinner's character for the imprisoned splendor of his nobler powers to come forth ?

The evangelism of Jesus is our answer to these questions. He knew what was in man. He understood the human soul. With the instinct of religious genius, he anticipated those insights into psychological law which have come to common men only after long and patient research. Therefore, modern science does homage to the method of the Master, seeing that its latest discoveries are but his primary principles. By way of illustration, rather than of exhaustive analysis, we may show how the evangelism of Jesus proceeded on three psychological principles that have, in recent years, come to be recognized as fundamental in all educational work.

The first of these is Suggestion. Professor Baldwin tells us that Suggestion in psychology means that all sorts of hints from without disturb and modify the beliefs and actions of the individual. He might have added that these hints do a large part of their work below the line of consciousness. For instance, a certain position in a certain little bed suggests sleep to a child; put him in that place and position, and in a little while, never thinking of sleep but counting his fingers or crooning a song, he falls asleep. Sometimes a tune keeps running in your head and you cannot imagine where it came from; note its time, and you will probably find that it was unconsciously started by a knock at the door, or the regular beating of your heart, or some other rhythmic movement or sound that had not fixed your attention.

Now the Incarnation, that is, the presence

of Jesus as the realized ideal of manhood in
the world, is the permanent Suggestion of
the higher life for man.   It works this way:
Christ came into the world and lived a faultless life.   Before him there had been theories,
visions, ideals of the perfect life; he made
the ideal a practical reality in the person of
a flesh-and-blood man.   Between him and
other ideals there is the difference between
the actual and the imaginary.   To see him,
therefore, awakens irresistible thought in a
man of what he himself may be.   Christ,
coming into the field of his consciousness as
a real person, not a dream, is the strongest
conceivable suggestion of the possibilities of
his own personality.   This suggestion, working even subconsciously, sets at work the
forces which shape his character into the
likeness of Christ.   It is maintained by
good authority, that it is the cherishing of an
ideal that gives unity to our consciousness.
We know ourselves in and by our ideal of
ourselves.   If this be true, how incalculable
is the formative power of the incarnate
Christ as the ideal of manhood constantly
present with men in a Christian land, even

in spite of themselves.   It sets even the sub-
conscious activities of the soul at work
making men Christlike.

The doctrine of the new birth receives
confirmation and illustration from the workings of psychologic suggestion.   The higher
possibilities of the soul lie dormant and do
not attempt to "open out a way" until they
are aroused from without; that is, until
something seen or heard or felt suggests the
exercise of these powers.   To illustrate from
lower ground, the instinct of fear is native
to every one; nobody could ever be made
afraid of anything if the instinct of fear were
not in him; but on the other hand, the instinct of fear never awakens until some suggestion of fear comes to the mind from
without; the child does not know what fear
is until all at once something frightful awakens the sleeping instinct.   Likewise the instinct of motherhood was doubtless a primary endowment of the first woman; but it
never awoke until there was a child to be
mothered.   The instinct of love resides in
the inmost sanctuary of each soul, but only
comes forth when an object of love is found.

So the divine life implanted by the Creator
in the soul of man lies slumbering there until it is awakened by the presentation of the
divine in Christ; his appearance is the suggestion that awakens it, and the response of
the soul to this suggestion, the coming forth
of the highest in us to meet the perfect in
Christ, is the new birth, the spiritual awakening; it is regeneration by the Holy Spirit.

The second great psychological principle
on which Jesus works is that of Imitation.
Imitation is a fact as old as mankind; its
psychological meaning has only recently
been investigated. Parents always knew
that children were mimics; it is only very
recently that the immense importance of
imitation in the development of the soul has
been recognized. When a child imitates, he
is doing nothing less than building his soul;
he is literally making himself. He is calling
forth his soul to self-realization by means of
his likeness to that which he imitates. He
is enlarging his self-consciousness to include
that of the dog or the horse or the man that
he mimics. He is finding that he is a self,

and that selfhood is essentially the same in him and in other persons. By his imitative games he builds into his soul an appreciation of the nature and value of the various trades and occupations, and learns to handle the materials of life as a master.

As we read the Gospels, it strikes us that imitation was the main reliance of Jesus, the fundamental and abiding method of his kingdom. God sent his Son in the flesh that men might have true "copy" to imitate; and one deep tone, thrilling through all the music of Jesus' words, is that which bids men be like him. Walking by the Sea of Galilee, he called his first disciples with the words, "Follow me"; and when all his teaching and training of his followers were completed, and, after the experience of death and resurrection, he stood again by the Sea of Galilee restoring the fallen fisherman, his farewell word to Simon Peter was, "Follow thou me." To be a Christian is to follow Christ; Christianity is just the imitation of Christ. The child by imitation of those whom he sees about him, builds his personality from the copy thus presented.

Even so we build our souls after the pattern presented in Christ. By conscious, resolute striving to be like him, we make his consciousness of fellowship with God, his conformity to the will of God, the reality of our inner lives. He is the Way; it is by imitating him that we open out a path on which the inner splendors of our souls may come forth.

The third great psychological principle in the Master's method of evangelism is that of education through Apperception of truth.

That the purpose of education is to call forth the native powers of the soul into the world of action, to open out a way for the imprisoned splendor to escape, is a familiar truism; but it is also true that this high purpose is often lost from view in teaching.

> " We teach and teach,
> Until like drumming pedagogues, we lose
> The thought that *what* we teach has higher ends
> Than being taught and learned."

The educational world has lately been much concerned with the doctrine of apperception. Apperception is a word to conjure with in these days. It really means nothing, as Professor James tells us in his "Talks to Teachers," but the way in which an idea is taken into the mind ; only, we must add, the doctrine of apperception has wholly changed our conception of the way in which an idea *is* taken into the mind. It used to be thought that when an idea was presented to the mind, the perceptive faculty laid hold of it, and passed it over to the memory for safe-keeping. Now it is known that no idea is ever taken into the mind that way ; a new idea does not find lodgment in the mind until the act of perception is followed by apperception ; that is, until the new idea is set in relation with the other contents of the mind. Ideas are social, never isolated individuals ; there is no such creature at large in the world as a man of one idea. No new idea can be imparted to the mind unless a "whole troop of ideas already present come forth to welcome it." What thus comes forth to welcome the new idea is often more important than that idea itself. The educational value of truth lies just in its power to call forth this response from within the soul. The educational value of any particular truth to any particular soul is here. To a mind just learning to count with numbers, the truth of ratio as expressed in the rule of three has no educational value, because there are no ideas in the mind ready to make friends and keep company with this new one. At a later time, when the properties of numbers are a little better understood, the truth of ratio will be educative, because it will be welcomed into the mind, associated with thoughts already there, and so understood. Education through apperception of truth means that the soul is developed, not by the impartation of truth as something from without, foreign to the mind, but by the response of the soul from within to the truth that is offered.

Now a review of the teaching and preaching of Jesus shows that he fully comprehended this principle, and worked upon it. He was never satisfied merely to declare the truth, nor did he have his followers repeat his statements of it after him until they were memorized. He strove in every way to get the truth understood, or apperceived.

He always sought to make connection between the new truth and the former contents of his hearers' minds. When he spoke
the Beatitudes, he dovetailed them into the
experiences of lowliness, sorrow and thirst
for righteousness that were present in the
minds of his disciples. When he interpreted
the duties of his kingdom, he grappled his
interpretation fast to the idea of law with
which they were familiar. When he would
impart a conception of the spiritual processes of his kingdom, he pointed to the
well-known figure of the sower in the field,
or to the woman with the measure of meal,
or to the fishermen drawing the net. In all
his teaching—difficult, highly spiritual, divinely mysterious as portions of it are—
there is everywhere the effort to secure the
apperception of the truth, to get his ideas
yoked together with the common stock-ideas
current in the minds of men.

That is why the gospel is the supreme
educational force in history. Men have
always wonderingly testified to the match-
less power of the gospel to draw out
the higher powers of the soul. Here is the

reason.   The gospel is educative because its Teacher put its truths before men in a form to be apperceived, to become not a part of man's mental store, but a part of his mental life.   The words of Plato are a priceless treasure, but the words of Jesus are spirit and are life.   The gospel is pure sunshine, drawing out what is in the soul as the sunlight draws the plant out of the seed beneath the soil ; out through the hard shell of the seed, up through the dark soil, the tender shoot pushes its way at the behest of the mighty sun ; so through the shell of a hardened heart, through dark masses of habits of sin, the spiritual life of man shoots forth in response to the gospel presented in Christ, coming forth from its prison to display its native splendor and worth, to blossom and flourish and bear fruit.

If we but understand him, we shall see that all the significant insights of modern psychology and pedagogy into the needs of the growing soul were anticipated by our Lord.   And the conviction on which the new evangelism must base all its work is that the method which Jesus, in the days of his incarnation, used for bringing men to God is the permanent method. The presence of the church (or, rather, of the Church) in a community, with its unceasing witness to the Master and his ideals, is the ever-present Suggestion to men of the higher life of the soul. Jesus himself, as presented by the Church in its teaching, and, more faintly but more vitally, in the lives of its members, is the perpetual object of imitation; the "Follow me" of Jesus is still the way to God. And the teaching of the Church, its preaching of the Word, its worship and sacraments, are abiding educational forces by which the truth is offered to men and elicits from their souls that response which brings out all that is best within. There may be many types of evangelism, many plans for bringing men to God; but the evangelism that follows Jesus must always be educational. Whatever form it may take, in gospel tent or stately cathedral, it never loses faith in the kingdom of God within the soul of man, or in the gospel of Jesus Christ as the power to bring that kingdom forth in splendid realization.

Educational evangelism holds that the gospel is not simply a message to men, but a power to generate righteousness in their souls and develop godliness from within; seeks not merely to tell men of Christ, but to build Christ himself—his consciousness of God, his union with the will of God—into the personality of men; is not content to be forever repeating the angels' song of peace on earth among men of good will, but says with St. Paul, " My little children, of whom I am again in travail until Christ be formed in you "; understands its mission to be not only to proclaim the good news of Christ, but, by applying its good news as a compelling, formative, educative power to the soul, to fashion the men of the world into the image of Christ.   This is an ideal, at once of evangelism and of religious education, which Jesus set forth in his practice, which the scientific interpretation of the nature of the soul and the meaning of the gospel for it supports, and which the Church is coming in our time more clearly to see, and more widely, deliberately and joyfully to accept.

CHAPTER VI

Personal Adjustment

ONE of the profound convictions in which modern thought has resulted is that the only way of well-being for any creature whatsoever lies through felicitous adaptation to its proper environment. Another conviction equally assured is that the life of a human being, with all its varied interests and activities, here and hereafter, forms a unity. Human well-being, therefore, requires the adaptation of men to their environment, and permanent well-being requires a complete and final adaptation of the total man to his ultimate environment.

What does salvation mean to men whose thoughts are cast in the most modern mold? To the practical man, to-day as always, salvation is the reformation of the outward life :—the prodigal forsakes his wanton wandering and returns home ; the wicked man ceases to do evil and learns to do well; the one who stole steals no more, but makes reparation; the hateful liar learns to speak the truth in love, and profane lips to utter the Holy Name in prayer; the stiff-necked infidel bows in worship, the scoffer becomes a learner, and the one who reviled the exercises of religion leaves his evil companions and goes rejoicingly to the sanctuary on the Lord's Day. To the mystic of to-day, salvation is an inward experience of indescribable delight, an inward peace, a transport of spiritual devotion, a bathing of the spirit in a sea of love, a rapturous assurance that we are in the hands of the Eternal who is our Friend, and whose friendliness is our pledge of all blessedness now and forever. To the theologian, now as ever, salvation is a divine intervention to rescue helpless sinners from a hopeless fate, the doing of a work which men could not do, a work of infinite mercy divinely brought to completion at Calvary, and being progressively developed in its effects upon men by the agency of the Holy Spirit in the hearts of all who are being saved.

But reflective men of the present, whose thinking, whether they will or not, is profoundly influenced by the evolutionary philosophy, are likely, in the effort to apprehend the reality for which the name stands, to conceive of salvation in other terms. The truth of the practical, mystical and theological views is not called in question ; but another view is found to satisfy our ways of thinking better. In this view, which may be called the psychological, attention is concentrated upon what takes place within the soul itself that is being saved. It has been said that Carlyle wrote history from a point of view within the actors ; the effort of much recent thought with regard to salvation is precisely to get this interior view, and describe the inward human reality of the process that sets a man right with God.

Viewed thus, salvation is seen to be the attainment by a human being of his final welfare by a proper adjustment of his entire nature to his total environment. The religious problem, therefore, the same for all ages but acutely accentuated in youth, is a problem in personal adjustment.

The supreme task at which Nature requires the youth to labor is the adjustment
of his personal life to the world-life. Whatever birth, heredity and training may have
done or not done for him, the imperious requirement of life is that he shall make this
adjustment himself, or at the least personally
ratify what has been done. The work appears in many phases ; the intellectual activities of youth have for their supreme object
the adjustment of the mind to the world of
truth ; the efforts of the boy to find his
work point to the adjustment of his life to
the economic order, his friendships and love-
making to his adjustment in the social order ;
the interest of the moral life of youth is
likewise chiefly in the discovery of a fitting
adjustment to the moral order, while religion
is the feeling of the soul after its abiding-
place in the Father's house. Like a piece of
intricate machinery, a human life can run
smoothly and effectively only when it is
properly adjusted ; there are many adjustments to make, and the tragedies that come
from maladjustment are numberless.

The commonest mistake of all is that of

supposing that a partial and temporary adjustment of life is a complete and final one ; as when a man is perfectly satisfied with himself if his life has got itself so fitted into the economic order that he is making money, or a woman has no plans for her life beyond the four walls of a happy home. For home and business, truth and right, economic and social systems, are but subordinate parts of a larger whole. We name this larger whole, which is the ultimate environment of man's life, the divine order. It is to this that he must adjust himself before a continuing blessedness can be assured him. The divine order is a supreme system which includes all that can affect human welfare, and organizes all things material and spiritual for the ultimate good of man. Until the adjustment of the personal life to this order is settled, nothing is settled. If a true and correct adjustment is made here, all is ready for a true and correct adjustment in every subordinate relation. The proper adjustment of life to this highest order is therefore man's first concern, and the ancient claim of primacy for religion among human interests stands unmoved.

Salvation, then, in terms agreeable to modern thinking, is the fitting and permanent adjustment of a human soul to the divine order that envelops all life; the soul that has found such adjustment is saved, here and hereafter; no other is. Or, to put the matter in another way, salvation is the making of a man into an effective personality through adjustment to those fundamental conditions of real effectiveness which are all summed up in the phrase "the will of God." Every soul is a center of personal energy, an original cause. The well-being of the soul depends upon its profitable and effective use of its inherent energy. A lost soul is one whose energy is dissipated and ineffective; a saved soul one that is realizing the full measure of its personal effectiveness within the eternal order, freely and efficiently applying its energy to a work that will have at the last a permanent worth for God.

Such effectiveness of personality is possible for a finite being only when the per-

sonality has found its fitting place and full
adjustment within the total order or system
of which its life is a little fraction. And
since it is the effectiveness of a free person
that is contemplated, the necessary adjustment to the divine order must be a free,
personal self-adjustment. Hence results
the conflict between human freedom and
divine authority, and the appearance of
maladjustment as a struggle of personal
human will against the will of God. Hence
it follows also that the true resolution of
this discord is man's free acceptance for
himself of the divine authority. For only
he is free who is in harmonious adjustment
with his environment; no human power is
effective unless it works in line with the
superior powers; the soul is liberated only
by conformity to its world; its energies are
set free, personal character made effective,
salvation realized, only by its willing adaptation of itself to the requirements of the
eternal laws.

This is the paradox of the gospel. The
soul's liberation for effective living can be
accomplished only through self-renunciation

and the acceptance of a Master; for his mastery is not restraint or bondage, but support and strength.

> "Oh, where is the sea?" the fishes cried,
>   As they swam the crystal clearness through;
> "We've heard from of old of the ocean's tide
>   And we long to look on the waters blue.
>   The wise ones speak of an infinite sea;
>   Oh, who can tell us if such there be?"
>
> The lark flew up in the morning bright,
>   And sang and balanced on sunny wings;
> And this was its song; "I see the light;
>   I look on a world of beautiful things;
>   And flying and singing everywhere
>   In vain I have sought to find the air."

What the water is to the fishes and the air to the lark, the spiritual order represented by Jesus Christ is to the soul of man; only men may not remain so blissfully unconscious of their environment, and "whosoever would save his life shall lose it: and whosoever shall lose his life for my sake shall find it" is the law of spiritual adaptation to environment which, in some form or other, must be obeyed by every soul that becomes an effective spiritual personality and is saved.

Nothing less than the happy adjustment of the total life of man to its ultimate environment can satisfy the conditions of man's well-being; nothing less can be salvation. It must be admitted that salvation so conceived is likely to appear to some practical-minded persons as a somewhat misty and remote concern. The actual, practical endeavor with which we are commonly employed is to adjust ourselves to the world of custom and convention in which we happen to live, to make ourselves effective and successful in that sphere of practical activity in which our work is done. Yet at this point we are to recall a marked feature of youth's estrangement— the rebellion of so many young people against conventions, their demand for a better reason than custom, which is, in effect, a demand to know the true order. By whatever terms we may express it, the fact beneath the experiences of spiritual and moral unrest in youth, and the distress and longings of seekers after salvation in later years, is the demand of the soul for right adjustment to that order of life which is actually supreme and divine, an adjustment that shall be final for time and eternity, and so bring peace and permanent satisfaction to the soul.

If, then, salvation is a free, full, final, personal adjustment to the divine order, it is manifest that in securing it the personal will is the paramount factor. Let other factors work with what force they may, the problem of the soul's salvation remains at center forever the same—to get men freely, willingly, gladly, to surrender themselves to the direction of a higher power; or, more concretely, to submit themselves to the Lordship of Christ. By whatever path a man may approach salvation, he will find it at last in a glad, energetic choice and appropriation of Christ and his character as his highest good in time and eternity, a choice that differs from mere reluctant consent to the truth and acknowledgment of duty as the sunlight differs from a flickering candle flame. That adjustment of life which brings it into line with God's order may be promoted by a thousand influences more or less effective, but it must be brought about at last by the decisive action of the man's own will.

What are we to do to help children, youths and men to make that decisive choice? Since adjustment to the divine order must be made by act of will, how are we to go about it to win the wills of men for God? The modern psychology of the will offers a significant suggestion.

The first proposition of recent psychology is that the soul in all its processes and manifestations acts as a unit. Beginning with the facts of consciousness and making critical observations of the changes that occur as sensations, thoughts, reasonings, passions and purposes go streaming through the mind, the most rigid analysis fails to divide the soul. The soul is not cellular in structure, is not made up of parts, great or small. The old psychology mapped out the geography of the soul, as it were, in the belief that the different faculties unite to constitute the mind somewhat as the different States unite to make up the Union. It was a fascinating analogy which found various faculties in the soul to do different things, as the body has eyes to see, ears to hear, and feet to walk. But present-day psychology has utterly abandoned this ground. The study of consciousness reveals no such division of function. There is one field of consciousness, and only one—in normal persons. And in this field of consciousness there is just one actor; one indivisible personal soul that throws himself as a whole into all his acts of perceiving, remembering, reasoning, feeling and the like. It is not memory that remembers, but the soul; it is not reason that argues, but the soul; it is not imagination that constructs, but the soul; it is not the will that decrees action, but the soul. The soul himself attends to all of these functions, delegating nothing to subordinate agents.

The bearing of this upon the problem of winning the will is plain. The will never acts alone; and the attempt to win the will without convincing the reason and satisfying the heart is vain. Whatever the freedom of the will may mean, it is certain that acts of will are never independent of other mental processes. The intellectual, emo-

tional and volitional activities of the soul
can be separated in thought, and must, for
scientific clearness of understanding, be distinguished; actually, they coexist and are
inseparable. Neither ideas alone, nor feelings alone, nor volitions alone, ever have
exclusive possession of the field of consciousness. Every act of will is conditioned by
all the thoughts and feelings present to the
mind, and by the tendencies, prejudices and
habits that have become characteristic of
the individual. The appeal to the will,
therefore, must be an appeal to the whole
mental and spiritual organization, the entire
soul.

Just what is needed to secure right action of the personal will appears more
clearly from these quotations from Professor James' popular "Talks to Teachers."
"All our deeds were considered by the early
psychologists to be due to a peculiar faculty
called the will, without whose fiat action
could not occur. Thoughts, impressions, being intrinsically inactive, were supposed to
produce conduct only through the inter-
mediation of this superior agent. Until

they twitched its coat-tails, so to speak, no
outward behavior could occur. . . . The
fact is, there is no sort of consciousness
whatever, be it sensation, feeling or idea,
which does not directly and of itself tend
to discharge into some motor effect. . . .
A belief as fundamental as any in modern
psychology, is the belief at last attained,
that conscious processes of any sort, conscious processes merely as such, *must* pass
over into motion, open or concealed." The
problem of right choice, then, is simply to
find and bring to the fore the right idea.
Sometimes the mind is hostile to that idea
when found, dislikes to entertain it, and a
resolute effort of voluntary attention is required to drag it into the focus of the field
of consciousness and keep it there long
enough for its effects to be secured. Once
brought, however, in this way to the center
of the field, and held there, the reasonable
idea will exert those effects inevitably, auto-
matically; for the laws of connection between our consciousness and our nervous
system provide for the action then taking
place. "If then, you are asked, In what

does a moral act consist, when reduced to its simplest and most elementary form? you can make only one reply. You can say that it consists in the effort of attention by which we hold fast to an idea which but for that effort of attention would be driven out of the mind by the other psychological tendencies there. To think, in short, is the secret of will."

The immediate connection between ideas and actions, thus established by modern psychology, is of the first importance for evangelism. It was formerly believed that thoughts arouse feelings and feelings appeal to the will as motives for action. That psychology was responsible for the preaching—and the still more feebly sentimental teaching—that depends upon emotional appeals for its effect upon the will. But feeling is not now regarded by psychologists as a consequent of thought and an antecedent of action, but as an accompaniment of both. Feeling is the mind's appreciation of its own activities or states, and it is just as true that we feel because we act as that we act because we feel. Feeling has no more immediate power over the will than thought, since every idea tends of itself to become an act without waiting for any mediation whatsoever.

The act of will by which a life is brought into adjustment to the will of God is not different in its essential features from the simplest ideomotor discharge. It is not to be conceived as a mighty effort of the self-determining faculty under stress of intense emotional excitement awakened by the sanctions with which some such appeal as "Choose you this day whom ye will serve" is enforced, but as the automatic consequence of voluntary attention given to the idea of personal fellowship with God until that idea has become winning, dominant, masterful. Whence it follows, as a regulative principle for evangelism, that the salvation of human souls is to be promoted chiefly by getting religious ideas into the focus of attention. The task of the preacher or the teacher who would win the wills of men is to get the right idea of personal relation with God into the focus of their consciousness, and hold it there until it produces the desired action. It is all a matter of sustained interest and attention. What people may feel is a question that may be left entirely out of consideration. Of course they will feel, and feel deeply, when great thoughts are adequately set before them; but they will act, not because of what they feel, but because the right idea of action has been held in the focus of their minds until the action becomes inevitable. The true preaching to the will is the preaching of ideas; or, better, the preaching of one idea at a time until the work of that idea is done. The effective preacher is not the one who moves his congregation to smiles or tears most readily, but the one who succeeds in grappling an idea drawn from the Word of God into the minds of his hearers, interlocking it with the ideas already there so that it becomes a permanent element of the mental life. Ideas so implanted determine conduct and character, and the preaching that effects this, accomplishes the one thing needful.

Our conception of the decisive act of will as the automatic result of ideas dominant in the mind is in no way modified by consideration of those cases of instantaneous conversion which are so impressive a feature of the history of religion, or of those other cases of prolonged struggles terminated at last by a single act of conscious volition. For the suddenness of the final issue does not prove the absence of that brooding over the ideas of religion which would normally result in such action. It is beyond a doubt that such brooding often takes place subconsciously. Ideas once lodged in the mind sink out of sight; but they disappear like seeds, to burst forth again with the surprising power of new life. A sudden conversion, or the sudden settling of a question long debated, is to be attributed, not to a simple, sheer, heroic decision, but to the sudden discovery of the full meaning and power of an idea perhaps long present to the mind, but hitherto disregarded. The result appears instantaneously, as a precipitate appears in a clear liquid the instant a certain chemical reagent is introduced; but as there is no precipitate unless the substance to form it is already there, although held in invisible solution, so there can be no conversion unless the soul has been made ready for it by the presence of specific religious ideas.

If a man is to act as a child of God, he must begin by thinking of himself as a child of God. It is in the effort of thought required to hold such an idea before the mind that men exercise " the will to believe." In order that the idea may work its appropriate result ; in order, for example, that the idea of a public confession of Christ may result in an actual confession of faith in him, it is usually necessary for the idea to be held prominently before the mind, to the exclusion of hostile and unsympathetic ideas, for a considerable period of time. Here is the psychological reason that makes special seasons of religious interest desirable. So occupied are people with other things, that it is exceedingly difficult to secure effective attention to religious matters unless they are set forth as the special subject for a given season. Hence, one day in seven is reserved as a time of rest from worldly work, and thought on sacred themes ; hence, churches endeavor, by the observance of Lent, and the Week of Prayer, by holding revival meetings, by appointing Decision Days, and similar methods, to secure continuous attention to the main ideas of religion until suitable action follows.

Such seasons are also agreeable to that law of the mind which decrees that interest, especially the collective interest of the community, shall come and go in waves. Waves of unusual religious interest are to be expected, just because religion is one of the concerns to which the minds of men return again and again. But when such a wave comes, religious leaders do well to remember that its value lies wholly in its effectiveness in fixing attention upon religious ideas. Except as it promotes earnest, sober, personal thought, it is likely to do more harm than good. No appeal is to be tolerated to anything less than the whole religious nature of men. The only converts worth having are those whose minds are satisfied as fully as their hearts. When revivalists learn to take advantage of these seasons of exceptional interest, not to appeal to the emotions and harrow the souls of men, or to urge, threaten or cajole them into "taking a stand" under the unusual pressure of the time, but to bring before their minds in the most winning way the richest, loftiest, sweetest truths of our religion, that they may come under the sway of splendid ideas and eternal verities, there will be fewer backsliders among the converts, and less ground for objection to revivals as a method of seeking to save souls.

But the unmistakable conclusion to which this line of thought points is that the most significant work that can be done to promote the salvation of men is the work of him who furnishes the young mind with its ideas of religion. The truths of the gospel, inwrought into the mind by methods that are in essence educational, are more efficacious in winning the wills of men than any other instruments whatever. This is the secret of the enormous power in all times of the faithful teaching and the instructive preaching of the Word of God. Christian culture, as distinguished from Christian nurture, is the work of holding before the minds of children, youths and men the essential truths of the Christian religion, in the confidence that these truths, when actually received into the minds of the hearers, will of themselves do the work of adjusting their lives to the divine.

Here is the splendid opportunity of the Christian teacher. The mind of youth picks up ideas everywhere—strange, fantastic ones, sometimes; the boy collects his notions about religion from parents, preachers, friends, reading, church services, a score of sources; but it is passing strange if the teacher to whom he brings his mind every week like an empty vessel to be filled does not furnish some of the greatest and most influential of them. The work of teaching is infinitely varied, its forms manifold. It is shared by every one who succeeds in clutching an important idea into another's mind, so that it becomes an operative part of his mental machinery. But whether done in the pulpit or the class-room or the home or the street, it is a work of unparalleled efficiency in adjusting youth to life. Let the truths of the gospel be actually taught, held in the focus of attention until they become an inalienable portion of the mental store, and their effect will duly appear in conduct and character. The Spirit waits upon truth so received, and God is pleased to impart the divine life to men by its means. And the conclusion of the argument is established beyond a doubt when we take the testimony of the Christian centuries; for excepting only a few short periods, they all agree that the teacher is the prince among evangelists.

CHAPTER VII

A Graded Gospel

THE evangelism that obeys Him who gave separate commands to feed the lambs and tend the sheep will provide a graded gospel. Only a gospel that is graded by the needs of the hearers can save those of different grades; only a gospel that grows with the growing soul can make Christian children into Christian men and women.

There is a type of evangelism that is too busy asserting its confidence in the power of the one old gospel to save all human souls to pay much heed to this requirement. Nevertheless, this long overlooked command of the Master is being forced into prominence. The demand for graded work in religious education has become too insistent to be longer ignored. The principle is winning recognition that the Church is bound to adapt its message to hearers of every stage of development as well as to those of every

146

race and kindred. A host of earnest men and women are laboring to put the religious training of the young upon a sound psychological and pedagogical basis, and to evolve a system that shall advance from grade to grade in accordance with established educational principles; already much has been accomplished, and the movement has gathered a momentum that will carry it to its goal.

Yet it may be modestly doubted whether, in general, the problem has been fairly grasped. Inadequate conceptions of the nature and aims of a true system of educational evangelism are responsible for much waste of energy and much inefficient work. Because of them many are doing the unnecessary and attempting the impossible. In particular, the analogy of the graded public school has been too strong for some, and the confusion of religious with intellectual education has led many astray. It may be well to keep up with the public schools, but it is not needful to ape their futile experiments, or be in haste to adopt methods which they are about to abandon. By all means, let the work of religious education be pursued by the most approved modern methods and take advantage of the experience of the day-schools; but let it not be imagined that graded Bible-schools and lesson helps, graded teaching of the contents of Scripture and the substance of Christian doctrine, insure the proper grading of the gospel. The fact must be admitted, for fact it is, stubborn and immovable as a rock, that the attempt to equal in the Sunday-school the thoroughness and efficiency in instruction of the public school is not likely to meet with general success until all the teaching is done by paid professional teachers and all the scholars are compelled to attend. And we can watch that expectation fade and vanish in the mists of immeasurable distance without regret, because such instruction, at the best, could make only good Biblical scholars, not Christians.

If the work of the Bible-school and kindred organizations is to promote in any effective manner that personal adjustment of the pupil to the divine order which is the chief, if not the only, object of religious education, the right principle must be found to govern the grading of the lessons and the construction of the system; and once found, it must be faithfully followed. At this point the present writer would imitate a well-known philosopher, and, foregoing all attempts to construct a perfect system or an ideal curriculum himself, would offer certain prolegomena to all future systems and curricula.

The grading of Biblical and doctrinal instruction is an important matter, but it is not the grading of the gospel. The intellectual elements of religion should be presented in appropriate connection and sequence to growing minds, but the emphatic demand of the present is for a properly graded presentation of the whole of religion to growing souls. The gospel itself, the good news embodied in Jesus Christ, has its appropriate grades for such presentation. It is these grades that educational evangelism must discover and put to use. Christian teachers must learn the difference between a course of graded Bible lessons and a graded gospel.

Educators have made a thorough study of

all the stages of the soul's development from infancy to age. At every stage the characteristic reactions of the soul, intellectual, emotional and volitional, have been noted. The pedagogical maxims that follow from the order of the soul's development have been carefully formulated, and the system of education framed in accordance with them.

At every stage of development, the soul has also its characteristic religious reactions. They are not the operations of a special faculty, but the reaction of the entire spiritual nature upon a certain kind of material. They therefore involve all the characteristics of the soul; they are conditioned by and akin to its intellectual, emotional and volitional characteristics. There is, as a consequence, a characteristic religion of childhood, of adolescence, of youth, of manhood and of age. There is also, we insist, a gospel, a characteristic Christian gospel, for each of these periods; a gospel designed by its divine Author to elicit wholesome and saving reactions in the growing soul at every stage.

It is true that there is only one gospel for Jew and Greek and barbarian, for child and youth and man. Yet the gospel for manhood does differ from the gospel for infancy. The difference is not in its content, its subject-matter; that is everywhere the same. The gospel is Jesus Christ, the Divine Person; that is the only gospel, and nothing else ever is gospel. The difference is in the appeal which this Divine Person makes to the soul. The gradation of the gospel is the gradation of its appeals. The divine personality, in order to impress itself upon a human soul, addresses itself now to one, now to another characteristic activity of the soul, as one or the other is dominant.

A Christian man's religion, from the point of view of psychology, is just the way his soul works upon the material of Christianity; that material is the divine life in the human, as presented in Jesus Christ. Religious education, if Christian, must therefore be the training of the soul to react correctly and effectively upon this material. And the one canon to guide the educator is that this material—the correct

material, the divine life in the world, God
in man—must be presented to the soul at
every stage of its development, in accord·
ance with its present capacity for correct
reactions, and as a stimulus to such reactions.   The instruction that presents Christ
in such a way is at once educative and
evangelistic.

What is meant by a graded gospel, then,
is this :—that the personality of Jesus, as the
union of man with God, is so presented in
the New Testament, and is to be so presented in Christian teaching, as to make a
fitting and effective appeal even to the soul
of the infant, eliciting a response marked
by the psychological characteristics of infancy indeed, but also characteristically
Christian, an infant's Christianity ; that
this divine personality, properly presented,
makes a like fitting and effective appeal to
childhood, evoking a reaction of the soul
that is characteristically childish *and* Christian ; that likewise from the souls of youths
and men it calls forth a response that in
every case combines the characteristics of
youth or manhood with those of Christianity,

The one business of religious education is to present Jesus Christ, and that for which he stands, life divine, human life divinized, in such a way as to call forth the fitting response of the soul at every stage of its growth.

As necessary prolegomena to any effective system of education in the Christian religion, we would therefore lay down the following propositions : that the essential subject-matter of religion is the union of man with God, that this subject-matter is embodied in the person of Jesus Christ, that his divine personality makes a distinctive appeal, which is religiously educative, to human souls of every degree of intelligence and at every stage of development, and that therefore the essential thing in any scheme of religious education is the proper presentation of the divine person, Christ Jesus.   It is evident that the very conception of religious education requires us to keep the evangelistic purpose to the fore ; how could it be otherwise ? For if education is the drawing out of the soul, can religious education be anything else than the drawing out of the soul to-

ward God ? That is evangelism, too. There
is a great deal of religious teaching that fails
to be educational just because it does not
draw out the soul toward God, but leaves
it as far from him as before.

What is the true order in the presentation of the Divine Person to growing
minds ?

St. Paul was wise enough to feed new
disciples with milk and not with meat. It
should need no argument to show that the
personality of Jesus cannot possibly mean
the same thing to infants and grown men, and
that children should not be schooled in the
religion of maturity. Common sense should
tell us, but it does not always, and proof has
been gathered by careful observers, that
children cannot possibly appreciate the
higher altruistic teaching of Christ or the
deepest religious experiences of men. To
train children to use the language and
imitate the experiences of adult religion
is to make them little hypocrites first and
great skeptics afterward.

But because the children cannot appreciate the highest reaches of the gospel,

it does not follow that the personality of
Jesus lacks all attractive force for them,
and that a scientific religious pedagogy requires all teaching concerning him to be de-
ferred to later years. It is not less of the
life and personality of Jesus that the little
ones need ; it is less of our mature thoughts
and theories about him.

The infant mind lies very close to God ;
the divine—not the philosophical Absolute
or the theological Infinite—but the divine in
the human, the God in Christ, is a natural
object of interest to it. The child looks
wonderingly but believingly upon the
marvelous workings of God in the world.
He loves stories, the more wonderful the
better, and stories are his proper spiritual
food. But the very foremost consideration in
the religious teaching of little children is this :
that no story, howsoever fascinating, has any
value whatever for purposes of religious
education unless it exhibits or illustrates in
some way the workings of the divine in the
human, God in the world and in man. That
God is working in this wondrous world
about us, that human life is all shot through

with glory by the unseen powers of divinity, that heaven lies about us in this world— that is a truth profoundly educative for infancy and early childhood. It is the truth which the Old Testament stories teach. It can be impressed by many stories from outside the Bible if caution be observed to make the line of distinction very plain between the stories that simply illustrate what might take place and those which teach that the true God did actually work as represented. Parables have their place, and fables, too. But teachers are never to teach as true what they regard as imaginative; if religion is not to be honeycombed with insincerity the tales of pagan superstition must not be put upon an equal footing in the child's mind with the records of Scripture; stories of the gods which Plato would not have in his Republic two thousand years ago may well be spared from Christian homes and Sunday-schools now. And by the same token, the teacher must distinguish among the stories in the Bible itself those that are to be taken literally and those that portray truths but do not represent facts.

The superlative stories for infancy and early childhood, which represent the workings of God in the world and in man most truthfully and most adequately, are the stories of Jesus. To tell them to little children, without explanation, theory or comment, is to make the most effective possible presentation of the great subject-matter of religion. They, better than anything else, make God real to the infant soul. Even those to whom the God of Abraham and Isaac and Jacob seems to be only a monstrous man, a magnified Power, understand that the God and Father of our Lord Jesus Christ is a loving person. Some things concerning our Lord's life and passion the little ones cannot understand; but if the object of religious education is Christian character, the child's mind cannot be too early supplied with the distinctive Christian material of religion, the old, old story of Jesus and his love.

After the first acquisitive, trustful years of early childhood, there comes a period of doubt. The mind begins to demand reasons and estimate probabilities. Things that cannot readily be understood are now often met with outright skepticism; and that, too, long before adolescent disturbances begin. In this period the miraculous element in God's dealings with men is likely to raise serious questions, and should not be unduly urged upon the attention. For another interest has come forward. The child is getting the outlines of that which is "everlastingly so" settled in his mind; and his incipient conviction that there is a law which changes not had best not be disturbed by apparent miraculous violations of law; for on the proper crystallization of this conviction the moral vigor of his spirit depends; he is laying the foundations of conscience.

The nature and importance of this process become more clear from the following consideration. Two kinds of relations make up our lives: necessary relations in which we stand by virtue of our humanity, and free personal relations into which we enter by choice. In childhood, attention is directed chiefly to the necessary relations. The child is here without choice of his own; he is busy learning that there is a world about him; he accepts what he finds. He learns that with his parents, his brothers and sisters, his home and general surroundings, he stands in relations over which he has no power.

Note now that it is in this region of necessary relationships that law and conscience are grounded. It is because certain things are necessarily so, that we are bound to make certain other things thus and so. It is because we stand in necessary relations with our parents that we ought to honor them. It is because we have necessary, unchangeable relations to universal principles of righteousness, that it is our duty to shun wrong and do right in each specific case. The period of childhood, therefore, when one is discovering these necessary relations and making himself familiar with the fixed points in the environment of his life, is the proper time for the unchanging certainties of the moral environment also to be learned, and the conscience to be formed. As a matter of fact, conscience is formed and fixed for life in most persons before they are twelve years old; only a great revolution can change it after that.

How shall educational evangelism deal with the conscience-forming period of childhood?

It is evident that before one can become a Christian, his moral nature must be set right. No one can be a Christian whose moral perceptions and convictions are all awry. St. Paul discovered that the law had been a schoolmaster to bring men to Christ. The divine in Christ can by no means be appreciated or held as an ideal, the meaning of salvation through Christ by no means understood, until the everlasting principles of right and wrong are estimated at their true valuation. Does not this require us to give the children a thorough course in the Old Testament before introducing them to the New, and show that the historical approach is the only true approach to Christ?

Such a plan has been suggested, and ably defended. But it is as far from the Christian method as Sinai is from Calvary. For the law on which a child's conscience is to be formed is not found in the Old Testament. We do not undervalue the Old Testament by insisting that it must be kept in its place; and that place is the region of foreshadowings in ethics as in religion. The conscience of Christian children is to be shaped not by Mosaic but by Christian ethics. Many of the moral precepts of the ancient law are adopted by the gospel without change of wording, and should be memorized by children as foundation materials for moral education. But the ethical principle of the Mosaic system cannot compare with the ethical principle of Christ in power to grip and hold and rectify the moral nature. The law of Moses rests on the divine command—" God spake all these words." The ethical principle of Jesus is the divine Fatherhood—every command and exhortation is referred to the wish or character of " your Father who is in heaven," and the reason urged for obedience is " that ye may be sons of your Father who is in heaven." The Christian conceptions of right, duty and law are based upon the fatherly relation of God to men. The

law which is now to lead our children to
Christ is the law that he came not to destroy
but to fulfil, namely, *not* the law given in
commandments and ordinances, but the
eternal law of the fatherly and filial relation
of God and man.

In developing the conscience of the child
by this law, there is a wide range of material to be used in moral instruction. The
most effective is that which presents con-
crete cases of good and evil deeds, the struggle of righteousness with sin, divine sonship
with human selfishness; stories which bear
their meaning home to the soul without any
hæc fabula docet, and elicit the fitting response of approval or disapproval from the
child's moral nature. By such exercise the
moral judgment is trained to act keenly,
promptly and decisively. And here again
one set of stories is preeminent. The stories
of the Ideal Man, the perfect Son, are peerless for the culture of the moral nature.
Among them there is one that transcends
all the rest. A hundred generations have
found that there is nothing else in all the
world that touches the conscience with so

sure, so safe, so masterly a touch as the story
of the Cross. The story of the cross of
Christ is the supreme power on earth for the
rectification of conscience. This, more than
all else, corrects errors in the moral view,
brings men into sympathy with the mind of
God, and makes them see the true nature of
moral offenses and the unspeakable worth
of holiness. In the presence of the cross of
Christ there is no room for casuistry or confusion. The child cannot understand the
atonement, and should not be asked to try.
But children can, and do, very early, catch
the meaning of the fact that Christ died for
the sin of the world; children can, and do,
very early, bring their moral natures to the
cross of Christ, and there begin to gain the
Christian insight into the great realities of
right and wrong, suffering and sacrifice, sin
and salvation.

Childhood learns the world, and conforms
to it. With adolescence comes the consciousness of a new self within the soul. The
necessary relations of life, having become
fairly familiar, retreat to form the back-

ground of consciousness henceforth, while a
new interest comes to the fore. The child
has been wonderingly learning to know the
world without; the youth is now amazed at
the world he finds within. The mysteries
of his own personality now challenge him
to search them out. He finds himself occupied with the problems of a free person.
He ceases to ask, concerning things, what
is; begins to think what may be, what he
can cause to be. Toward persons he begins
to act as a person, no longer imitatively, but
freely, independently. Personal interests
now become the supreme concern of his life.
In early adolescence, this main concern is
largely self-centered. The youth is learning
to know himself; his spirit is distinctly anti-
social. But with self-knowledge comes a
new interest in what life and truth shall
mean to him, and he passes into the second
period of adolescence. He now shows that
he is no longer a child by declining to appropriate without reserve everything offered
to his mind; he begins to sift and sort
and separate; discriminates, questions, grows
more positive of his beliefs and disbeliefs.

His mind takes up the higher rational processes, and insists on having reasons, evidence, proof. He declines to believe on the
authority of others, unless he has full confidence in their veracity; declines to act on
the direction of others, unless he is fully
assured of their wisdom.

In the later period of adolescence, the
youth discovers that he is a member of
society. His intellectual unrest is accompanied by feelings, emotions, aspirations
hitherto unknown, that carry him out of
himself. Conscience, now well-defined in
character, broadens its reach, and the moral
imperative bears down upon the soul of
youth with a weight never felt when the
child obeyed superiors without question and
without responsibility. As a child, this
youth was cared for; now he must begin to
care for others. Boys and girls leave school
to become breadwinners. "Not to be min-
istered unto, but to minister," takes on for
them the dead-earnest meaning of real life.
The self-centered life of the child is being
transformed into the socialized life of the
man, and the claims of the social order are

one by one enforced upon him.   The strongest of all the forces that work to this end comes into play when the differentiation of the sexes is complete and each begins to feel the attractions and realize its own need of the other.   At last the process by which youths and maidens are naturalized in the social world—that is, the world of persons—reaches its culmination, when, after the years of storm and stress, of distrust and bashfulness, perhaps of flightiness and frivolity, they settle down as heads of families, accepting in marriage the full social obligations of maturity.

Thus nature has ordained that the normal business of youth shall be to find one's true place in the world of free persons.   Just as physical development is the main interest at one period, so personal and social relations become the supreme concern at another. What is the vanity of youth, but just an expression of the new consciousness of

> " This main miracle, that thou art thou,
>   With power on thine own act, and on the world " ?

What is youth's sentimentalism, but a sense

of the value of personality with its purposes
and passions, exaggerated because it has
just come into the field of vision and fills it
completely ?

The long and passionate struggle of a
youth's restless years is to get a correct adjustment of personal and social relations
with the persons who make up the human
world about him, and the Supreme Person
above. On correct adjustment here, the
blessedness or the perdition of life depends ;
the burden of responsibility cannot be
shifted ; each must make his own adjustment, with fatal results for weal or woe ;
and that is why the hopes of youth are such
bounding hopes, the sorrows of youth such
poignant sorrows.

Youth, then, is the normal time when one
should " experience religion." Morality is
an interpretation of the necessary relations
of the soul ; the moral idea is that of happy
conformity to that which is essentially so.
But religion is characteristically personal, is
an interpretation of personal relations ; the
religious idea, as distinguished from the
moral, is that of harmony between free per-

sons, right personal relations between man and God. Since relations of this kind form the foreground of the thought of youth, the soul is clearly ready for the distinctively religious appeal.

The Christ for youth is the Christ who enters into free relations with men; who walked and ate and talked with men, received their homage and relieved their pain, instructed their minds and forgave their sins; who was loved by John, denied by Peter, betrayed by Judas, condemned by Pilate, and worshiped by Mary; who bids men enter into life by the narrow gate, deny self, take up the cross, leave all and follow him. The aggravated self-consciousness of youth implies a potential corresponding consciousness of the worth of other selves; the youth knows how to do and suffer for another. He is ready for the altruistic teaching of the gospel; losing life that it may be saved now comes to have a real, clear meaning for him. In all the world of persons to whom life may be devoted, Christ appears as supreme, the One above all others to be believed in, trusted, loved and served; the one entirely worthy Master of the soul, to die for whom is gain.

Of the presentation of Christ to the souls that are mature, it need only be said here, that these souls have reached the time for life's work, and the Christ that appeals to them is Christ the Worker. The religion of service is the religion for manhood. Conscience has been developed, personal relations largely settled, personal habits made stable, life's calling found, one's home fixed; now there is work to do! The soul of the man who does his honest share of the work of the world needs often to see Jesus working his divine work, offering to God his faithful service, blessing the world by his toil and pain and sacrifice. The heroic in Christ calls forth the manly in men, and is educative until life's work is done.

Since the Church, willingly or not, is definitely committed to the methods of educational evangelism as the chief means of winning men to God, its greatest need is skill, guided by the Holy Spirit, in handling a graded gospel. Those who are skilled to present Christ adequately and appropriately to human souls of every grade—or of one particular grade—are in demand. Great progress has been made in recent years, but yet how many Sunday-school teachers are there who really understand the characteristic differences between infancy, childhood and youth, and know how to change the appeal of their teaching at just the right stage of growth ? How many, for example, know how to teach the Ten Commandments to children as an expression of the highest right, the will of a Father to be implicitly obeyed ; and then how to set those same words before youths as an expression of the Highest Person's mind, the terms of right relations and happy fellowship with him ? It is because of failure to understand the grading of the gospel that the appeal to the higher personal consciousness is so often offered to little children who cannot possibly —for physiological as well as psychological reasons—comprehend it; and it thus becomes wretched cant and driveling sentiment on the lips of the teacher ; and on those of the children, if they take it up, soul-deadening hypocrisy. How often boys at the period of adolescence grow weary of the Sunday-school because their teacher does not know any better than to continue with them the moral appeal of childhood ! It was the best thing possible for them two years ago, but is now become a barren platitude, mere goody-goodiness, because their souls are ready for a deeper, personal religion.

In that reorganization of the evangelistic methods of the church which is so urgently demanded, the very first step is to learn the distinctive appeals of the Divine Person which are effective at the different stages of the soul's development. When they have been mastered, graded instruction in the contents of the Bible and the doctrines of the faith may well receive attention. But no religious instruction will possess permanent attraction and interest for human souls if it fails to hold before them all the time the fundamental religious truth, the divine in the human. Stories may interest little children for a few years—any kind of stories ; picnics may keep the boys in school a little longer—any

kind of picnics. But the men of our day
are in more serious business than being entertained with stories and picnics; and
they will surely not be found in the church
or Sunday-school that fails to supply the
hunger of their souls for the divine fellowship by making the one supreme religious
idea of the union of the earthly with the
celestial—the divine life in man, God in the
world, the Son of God incarnate—central in
all its teaching.

CHAPTER VIII

The School of Worship

IF there is one thing that the churches of America are trying with all their human might to do, it is to enroll all their children and young people in Sunday-schools, Young People's Societies, or kindred organizations, and keep them there until they are ready to unite with the church.

They cannot do it. They never will be able to do it. And there is a good reason why.

The reason is not the inefficiency of the Sunday-schools. We are not about to launch out in a criticism of them. They are not perfect, but they are the greatest adjunct of the church in this age. The faith that men show in the Sunday-school as the leading institution in the American system of religious education, and their determination to improve it, are among the most encouraging features of the present situation. We are not here concerned, however, to discuss the Sunday-school or any other form of organized religious work, but only to comment on the behavior of youth toward the institutions of religion, and to inquire what that behavior means.

Let us put together two of the best known facts in this field. The first is the disposition of the larger boys—and girls, too, in a slightly less degree—to leave the Sunday-school during adolescence. The Sunday-school gets and interests the children. In most communities, there is little occasion to raise the question how to get the children into the Sunday-school. They are already there—some of them in two or three schools. We hear of multitudes who do not attend church; but their children do attend our Sunday-schools. But beyond the age of childhood we cannot keep them. About the age of twelve they begin to get restless, and in a few months or years the most of them are gone. Nor have we devised any effectual means of inducing them to stay. There are exceptional teachers, who by exceptional means hold exceptional classes together. There are other classes that simply cannot be held. We have our Junior Societies and Leagues; it is easy enough to attract large numbers of children to them; but they are conspicuously unsuccessful in graduating boys of fourteen to sixteen years into the senior societies. We organize Boys' Brigades, Sunday-school baseball teams, and so on; and the very boys for whom we plan them ridicule the whole thing. It is probable that, in general, the great majority of the children under fourteen are in some Sunday-school or children's religious society, while a clear majority of youths of both sexes from fourteen to twenty-one are not in any Sunday-school or religious society. A certain proportion remain; but with regard to the majority, it is not difficult, it is impossible, to keep them in Sunday-school, Young People's Society, or any kindred organization.

There is one fact; now consider the other. It has long been customary in revival meetings to warn people against delay by an exhibition of the comparative numbers who begin the religious life at different ages. The evangelist asks those converted before they were twenty to rise and three-fourths of the congregation rise; he asks those converted after forty to rise, and there are only a handful. The argument is unanswerable. In more recent years, the age of conversion has been made a matter of scientific study, and all are now familiar with the statistics collected by President G. Stanley Hall and his followers, showing that nearly all of those who ever become members of the church are converted and join the church between the ages of twelve and twenty. This is the second fact. Put the two together; the result is amazingly worth our attention; the age at which the Sunday-school loses most is the age at which the church gains most. The time of exodus from the Sunday-school is the time of ingathering for the church. The period of alienation and estrangement, when the big boys and girls forsake the Sunday-school and similar organizations is the very time when they

flock to join the church.   What is the meaning of this ?

Some would dismiss the matter by.saying
that it simply means the separation of the
religiously inclined from those who are not
so.   Those who care nothing for religion
leave the Sunday-school and other religious
services, while those who remain in the
Sunday-school and Endeavor Society become members of the church.   There is
much truth in this view ; but not enough
truth to explain our facts.   For what proportion of the members of the church are in
the Sunday-school ?   Suppose we say one-
third, which is surely a generous estimate.
The fact then remains that two-thirds of
the confessedly religious people, those who
become members of the church, do not
keep up their connection with the Sunday-
school.

The true explanation lies deeper.   In our
study of that dramatic action through
which a soul passes on its way from childhood to maturity we have found a constitutional reason for these facts.

We have seen that youth is the time when

the soul finds itself, and that the essential
features of the process of self-discovery are
alienation and return. The youth realizes
the meaning of his individual personality by
setting himself over against his environment; questioning, experimenting, investi-
gating, in order that his convictions may
rest upon his own experience and his life
become self-governed. With some temperaments, as we have seen, this process involves
a radical and sweeping change, a sometimes
violent throwing off of home restraints and
influences, a strange turning against things
loved in childhood, an unsettling of the
whole moral and spiritual life. With any
temperament, there is a tendency for the
boy to become self-conscious, bashful, secretive; he dreads to be questioned or pressed
closely; will not speak, if he can help it, of
his most intimate thoughts; refuses to exhibit his heart to any one.

He ceases to go to Sunday-school because
his nature shrinks from the close personal
touch with the truth and the teacher in the
presence of others which a small Sunday-
school class involves. He will avoid his

pastor, father, mother, or any one else likely to speak to him of religious things, because his whole soul resents interference with its God-given privilege of discovering life for itself. The only one who can win his confidence, is the one who understands him without saying so, and forbears to intrude upon his private thoughts. He declines to take part in a prayer-meeting, because he is not ready to speak of his own new spiritual experiences; he really does not know what to say, for he is so unsettled. And those who say that he ought not to be so unsettled, simply do not understand youth, and are impertinent meddlers with God's and Nature's ways.

But none the less, "the thoughts of youth are long, long thoughts." The adolescent mind is keenly sensitive to spiritual truth. No one is more deeply, passionately interested in the good, the right, the true and the beautiful. The boy's mind is warm and fertile soil, all ready for the good seed and thirsting for the water of life to make it grow. Life and what to do with it, love and its meaning, self-sacrifice and the splen-

dor of it, are the familiar thoughts of the
adolescent boy. He demands reality and
not make-believe, substance and not show,
the perfect and not the defective, the whole
and not a part. That is why you cannot
save him with a fragment of the gospel
or satisfy him with a fraction of the church
life. That is why this boy who has grown
tired of the Sunday-school despises the pastor or parent who hopes to make him religious with a Boys' Brigade or a ball-team.
That is why all methods that appeal to anything except the highest in him are doomed
to fail. Unwilling to express himself about
religious matters he undeniably is; irreligious he emphatically is not.

What he needs is a place where, all unquestioned and unobserved, he may lift up
his heart to God and give wings to his aspirations; where, without being hastened
or pressed, yet with wise help and guidance,
he may think out his long thoughts until
they settle his character for life. We are
often in too much haste to secure a confession, and the allegiance of the youth to an
institution of religion; God's way is to build

character, and to trust a character built on
Christ to make its own confession before the
world.

That place which the boy needs, God has
provided for him.   It is the service of worship where the Word is preached.   When
all other expedients have done their utmost,
they but make it increasingly clear that the
supreme institution for religious education
is that School of Worship, which in some
form or other has existed ever since the first
rude altar of stones was built, and in which
God, not man, presides over the religious
education of his children.

Observe how the service of this place suits
the soul of youth as though designed expressly to meet its needs.

The spiritual unrest and turmoil, the
undefined feelings and vague longings for
a life larger and more beautiful than yet
realized, the aspirations of the soul, its
hopes and fears and passions, all so keen,
so fresh, so wondrous, so little understood
by the new-born adolescent, prepare him
to see in the service of worship, with its
ritual and symbol and sacrament, a world

of rich meaning and deep satisfaction for his uneasy spirit. Let the emotions that make youth restless and fickle and sentimental be understood, and it will be clear that there is nothing in the wide world so fitted to satisfy and regulate them as a church service of worship. Again, the new independence in thinking, the impulse of the adolescent mind to work vigorously along the higher reaches of rational exercise, just fit him to follow and appreciate the continuous discourse of sermons. Now, if ever, the mind develops the power to think connectedly, and learns to take delight in discursive thought. And again, the adolescent impulse to social life, the passion to be like and with mature persons, which takes offense at the suggestion that a youth's place is with the children or in some corner by himself, is satisfied when the boy takes his place among grown-up worshipers in the house of God; while the youthful shyness that seeks concealment feels no violence done to it when the youthful worshiper worships unnoticed by men as one of a congregation. Thus the service of the church answers the needs and

processes of the adolescent soul as deep call-
eth unto deep; and in these youthful years,
or never, will he form the habit of regular
and appreciative attendance on worship and
sermons.   If, as a child, he has been present
at these services, he has neither appreciated
the liturgy nor understood the sermons; in
a few years, as a man, he will have no use
for either if they fail in these sensitive adolescent years to find and hold him.

What, then, is a truly educational evangelism to do for the youth? Does not the
finger of God, revealed in the nature that
he has implanted in the soul of youth, give
direction that when this time of alienation
comes, our effort should be to make these
young people at home in the services of the
church, rather than to keep them in the
children's place or put them off in an organization by themselves? Is not our failure with them largely due to our misunder-
standing of the real needs of their spiritual
natures? With certain temperaments, including a large proportion of the boys, the
ordinary methods of Sunday-school and
Young People's Society and like associa-

tions are utterly opposed to the processes of adolescent growth. To hold such youths in the Sunday-school may be to do violence to their spiritual natures,—to work, not with, but against, God in their souls. And let it be remembered that. every method or agency used in religious work must give account to God not only for the souls whom it wins and saves, but also for all whom it alienates and destroys. That some methods widely used do needlessly and cruelly drive men from the church and harden them against religion, is a fact beyond the possibility of doubt.

Be it distinctly understood that these words are not written in criticism of Sunday-schools, Young People's Societies, boys' clubs, and like agencies, but in rebuke of the stupidity that imagines that these agencies will accomplish the all-important things. Nearly all the young people who join the church come from the Sunday-school or Young People's Society; that is an unquestioned fact, and is as it should be; let it stand. But it is passing strange how any, even the well-known wayfaring man, can

miss the other fact, that all these agencies
have few, if any, converts to report where
adolescent boys and girls do not attend
services of worship and preaching. Give
all due credit to every agency that helps,
but let not the helper claim to be the master
workman. The services of worship represent the most efficient institution for the
development of the religious nature, the
education of human souls for God, that the
Creator has been able to bring forth upon
this earth after dealing with hundreds of
generations; and what a comment it is on
human folly, that when men set themselves
to devise a system of religious education
they practically ignore this institution in all
their discussions!

That church, we hold, is making a fatal
blunder which places its chief dependence
for the winning of the youth on any special
means outside its own services. Supplement
those services as you will; but once give a
boy to understand that he is such a peculiar
creature that a special place apart from the
men and women has to be provided for him;
give him the impression that you have no

hope of making a Christian man of him by
the regular God-appointed means, and you
have done him the last irreparable injury
for which no effort or sacrifice on your part
can atone.   And is not this precisely the
impression made by some of our present
methods ?   We hustle hither and thither,
and busy ourselves with everything else except showing the boys their place in the
church itself.   We send them to Bible
classes, urge them to join this club or that
association, go about all sorts of circui-
tous ways to catch by guile those who,
above all things, love directness and are
glad to be won by sincerity.   But, in most
churches, who thinks of interpreting the
service of worship to the youth, showing
them how to enter into it, how to make
public praise and common prayer the wings
of their own spirits to lift them up to God,
how to find in anthem and hymn and psalm
and Scripture and sermon the bread and the
water of life ?   Who does anything to make
them feel that the service is for them ?   So
long as we, by conduct and method and
organization, often, too, by outright asser-

tion, give the boys to understand that we expect them to get their religious culture and inspiration from some other source, how in the name of reason can we expect to find the men in the church ?

Parents and pastors should leave off their busy scheming and faithless worrying about the boys, and take time to ponder these facts in their hearts :—That Jewish law and custom required parents to take their twelve-year-old boys, not to some place prepared for the boys alone, but to the great temple at Jerusalem, the center of the religious life of the whole people ; that Jesus, going thus to the temple at twelve years of age, found, to his unspeakable delight, that it was his natural and fitting place, so that he wondered that his parents should look for him anywhere else ; that we, like the learned doctors there, would be amazed at the understanding and answers of our twelve-year-old boys, did we but take pains to discover their real thoughts of religious truth ; and that the place of the big boy, with his enlarging life and his passionately aspiring soul, is not necessarily in the Sunday-school

or the boys' club, which may indeed do
something for him, but is necessarily in his
Father's house, which will do all for him.

We can well afford to let everything else
wait until pastors and people have attended
to this matter of securing the attendance of
the young people of from twelve to twenty
at the services of worship where the gospel
is preached, and have provided there those
varied, rich and inspiring elements of worship, and that simple, manful, luminous,
convincing testimony to the truth which
the adolescent soul demands. For whatever other methods may be employed, our
hope of sound, intelligent conversions, of
lives devoted to the Master and characters
built on him, centers there.

It might seem to some that the confirmation system of the historic churches precisely meets the situation here developed;
for it is a great, regular, established, institutional effort to bring the adolescent children into the church itself. It has not only
centuries of Christian practice to commend
it, but the practice of Jews and pagans as

well.   The instinct of humanity has given
its voice in favor of some recognized method
of initiating the adolescent youth into the
sacred rites of his people.   Some such established practice is necessary to any complete system of educational evangelism.
The churches that practice confirmation are
not disposed to abandon it; and under
various names and forms, such as catechetical classes, pastor's classes, and the like,
which offer special instruction for those
about to join the church, its essential
features are rapidly coming back into the
churches where it has been supplanted by
the methods of the revival system.

Yet confirmation, as commonly practised,
is by no means an ideal method in religious
education.   The old objection is still valid
that it tends to formality, emphasizes the
intellectual rather than the vital, and makes
too little of the personal decision to live
the Christian life.   But a far more serious
difficulty is that children are usually confirmed too soon.   It is a dangerously easy
thing to take children in whom the new life
of adolescence is not fully awake, teach

them a catechism, persuade them that they ought to become communicants, and receive them into the church. What is accomplished by this? The one thing made perfectly certain is, that the church itself, its services and its communion, have been placed among the things from which the adolescent youth will soon feel himself estranged. The fact that they are communicants doubtless helps to hold some few steady through the storms of youth; but even these few are compelled to raise the question of the meaning and value of their church-membership, and very large numbers simply withdraw from active participation in the church life, because they now realize that they became communicants without understanding what it meant. Thus early confirmation defeats its own object. If the church is to have the personal loyalty of its members—and why should they be members on any other terms?—it is far more consonant with the laws of the soul's development that church-membership and communion should, as a rule, be among the things on the farther side of youth's estrangement, and be regarded, like citizenship, marriage, and business or professional life, as elements in the new, higher life that opens up to a young man when the disturbances of early adolescence are past.

To speak the truth, there is a bane of brevity that rests on most of our plans for bringing young people into the church. They lack the ordered continuity of purpose and effort essential to the promotion of vital religious advancement. There is no short cut from childish to mature faith. Nature takes ten years to do her special work in the soul of the youth; can the church expect to do hers in ten days or ten weeks? To receive children into the communion of the church just at the dawn of that period when their anti-social instincts awake, and then to think that they are safe, and ignore their special needs during the disturbances that are sure to follow, is only botching the work. And we have seen that it is a sore delusion to imagine that the situation can be adequately met by the formation of Young People's Societies, or any expedient of that kind. A true educational method must walk patiently by the side of youth through all the steps of its progress, recognizing its right to be anti-social—against all societies—at one time, welcoming the appearance of the gang spirit as a sign of a new social impulse, confident that the higher social instincts will assert their power later on, sure that the first thing is to keep the youth's place in his Father's house always ready for his return, careful above all things that he shall not be made to feel that he is utterly lost to religion and the church because he rebels against conventional forms and insists on going his own way for a time.

If it is true, as is asserted, that an increasing proportion of young men do not attend or support the church, may not one reason be the failure of the church to minister understandingly and fittingly to them in youth? This is indeed a large subject, not to be disposed of in a few sentences. The following suggestions are not made in the spirit of one who would lightly heal the hurt of Israel, but as matters that must be duly considered if the situation is to be fairly met.

1. We must deal with youth in vital, not formal, ways. They are to be regarded, not as factors in the parish organization, but as actors in its life. The very first thing required is that the church itself shall take cognizance of its youth; as a worshiping body, it must be aware of them, sensitive to their presence, responsive to their needs. Youth should be in our congregations as in our homes; their place is not the nursery, but the family living-room. There is no call to order either the church or the home life entirely to suit them, for they are only a part of the family, but it is a righteous demand that they shall not be ignored.

2. It would be natural to say, in the next place, that the church services should be adapted to youth; but this has been already done. No violent reconstruction of our methods of worship, no radical change in the style of preaching, is required by the interests of youth; all that is necessary is to be true to the ideals now cherished. The nearer we come to the ideal church service, the nearer we come to what youth wants. Dull sermons, tedious prayers, "balloon-

ing" by the choir, are no more profitable
for age than for youth. But the perennial
freshness of the gospel imparts a youthful
spirit to the very nature of Christian worship. We all go to church to have renewed
in us the hopefulness and confidence, the
courage and assurance, the fresh enthusiasm
and glad anticipations, that are youth's own
property. Surely if this atmosphere is in
the service, youth will feel at home there.
And when it comes to the teaching, the
doctrine, the sermon, there is hardly a
greater homiletic mistake than to suppose
that the best thought of a mature mind
presented in the most effective way to reach
earnest men is not the proper food for the
youth. Children's sermons may be very well
for children now and then, but they are an
abomination to boys in long trousers; what
they need is the preacher's best thought,
put in his most businesslike way. If a
sermon is prepared for those who are fond
of some special type of thought or method
of discourse, it is likely to miss the youth;
but not if it is a vital utterance of substantial truth addressed to serious men and

women.   That is all youth asks, for it is what youth loves.

3.   Perhaps the greatest need of all at present is a concerted and continuous effort on the part of pastors, parents, pewholders, Sunday-school officers and teachers, and all concerned, to secure the attendance of the youth at the church services.   Many Christian people thoughtlessly allow their children to grow up without forming the habit of attending church; the Sunday-school or children's society is considered enough for them, until suddenly it appears that they do not want to go to any religious service. In many, if not most, Sunday-schools there are children whose parents do not attend church, so that they are not likely of themselves to form the church-going habit.   In some places the free-seat crusade has wrought havoc with the idea that a whole family should sit together in their own pew, and the younger members have felt free to sit where and come when they pleased.   So it has come to pass that there exists in almost every parish a considerable number of boys and girls between twelve and twenty

years of age who have never learned to attend the church services or enter into its worship, although in a very real sense they belong to that parish. The church itself must go after these young people; under no circumstances are they to be committed to the care of any subordinate organization. They are in their golden age, and they form the church's golden opportunity. Nothing else in its work is so promising. It may be a church that occupies a position of commanding influence, and has heavy duties in leading the thought and shaping the moral sentiment of a large community, but it will lose nothing of influence or standing if it brings all possible resources to bear upon the problem of securing the regular attendance and the reverent attention of these young people at its services.

The effort will call for patience. Some of these young people will assert their independence in perverse and exasperating ways. Disappointed hopes are familiar inmates of every heart that deals with youth. But those who drift out of Sunday-school and seldom or never attend church are not to be given up.   They are to be followed with a care as faithful and a love as true as though they were already communicants of the church.   If we were less hasty and impatient, less ready to cross their names off our lists and our memories when they turn their backs upon us, perhaps fewer young men would remain in the far country of estrangement from the church.

4.   If the church is to command the respect of youth, church-membership should be held before them as an ideal for maturity.   There are exceptional children who should be received into the church very early, and it is an unwise course to put off any who manifest a really intelligent desire to become communicants.   But the man who defers church-membership until the follies of youth are past is in a more hopeful spiritual condition than the one who went through it all in childhood and considers it a thing outgrown.   The very heart is taken out of youth if it have not something to look forward to.   In religious matters, as in others, it is a mistake to deprive young people of the privilege of anticipating

things which the older people enjoy but which are still denied to them. Too often the spirit of " 'T is done, the great transaction's done" takes possession of the boys and girls that have been received into communion, and their development is arrested because they have been admitted too early and too easily to the highest privileges of church life. Sixteen to twenty years is in general the best age for young people to join the church; and then they are not to come in as those who have already attained, but as those entering a race, determined to press on to a goal clearly seen but not to be reached without earnest effort.

5. Finally, in all dealings with young people, it is necessary to bear constantly in mind the distinction between personal and institutional religion. That is not first which is institutional, but that which is personal; then that which is institutional. Youth's first task is to achieve a personal religion. In doing so he is very likely to undervalue religious institutions. He will probably affect to be able to do without them for a time; he may boast that he can

find and worship God as well by other
means. It may be that he must learn some
lessons in the school of life before he is prepared to acknowledge his debt to the institutions of worship. But if he seriously takes
those lessons to heart, he will come in time
to see the value of the church to society and
to himself. He will learn that human welfare is essentially a social thing, and no man
can be saved outside the Christian community. He will find that the very things
among his own spiritual possessions on which
he prides himself most are his only by virtue
of his place in a Christian society, so that he
must ask himself, What hast thou that thou
hast not received ? And he will discover
that, next to the school of life, the school of
worship is the educational center for God's
discipline of human souls. There, under the
tuition of the heavenly influences that are
exercised by devout prayer and lofty praise
and reverent meditation, the soul is led most
surely forth to meet its God ; and he who
once has learned, in the school of life, to say
from the heart, " I love thy kingdom, Lord,"
is likely to go on, as the years of sweet and

sober experience add their touches to his spirit and finish its education, and say,

> " I love thy church, O God.
>
> *   *   *   *   *
>
> " Beyond my highest joy
> I prize her heavenly ways,
> Her sweet communion, solemn vows,
> Her hymns of love and praise."

CHAPTER IX

Aims and Expectations

IT was to be expected that the study of adolescence, which has attracted so much attention in recent years, would issue in valuable practical suggestions for the guidance of those who deal with youth. Nor has it been barren of such issue ; many of its findings are already the commonplaces of educational literature. No other portion of this field of research, moreover, has possessed such compelling interest or been so richly fruitful as that which deals with the religious experience of youth. A new vision of the meaning of religious work for youth has been opened to men, with new renderings of the aims, ideals, expectations, materials and methods of religious education. Our next task will be to develop, from that course of spiritual development which has been shown to be typical of adolescence, certain working principles as to the aims and expectations in accordance with which religious work for youth is to be conceived and organized.

Since youth stands by itself as a period of life unique in significance, the aim of religious work for youth is to be sharply distinguished from the aim of religious work for childhood or maturity. The distinction is found in the necessity for the complete fusion of the evangelistic and educational ideals for youth. With men they are divided. Those who are mature in character and settled in habit are treated as either believers or unbelievers. Religious work for them proceeds upon the assumption that they have either some established personal faith to be developed and encouraged, or a settled unbelief not easily overthrown. The object of religious work for men is correctly enough divided into two departments according to the old program—to convert sinners and edify saints. To children, however, this distinction is not properly applied. They are not as yet either believers or unbelievers, Christians or skeptics, saints or sinners.

They are the subjects of a religious development that has only begun. The object of religious work with children is to promote that development, postponing the attempt to separate believers from unbelievers until years of discretion are reached. The distinctive aim is to draw out the religious capacities of the child by impressing him deeply with the objective realities of religion—the being and fatherhood of God, the life and sacrifice of Christ, the fundamental requirements of the moral law and the Christian life.

Now the youth are like children in that they are not to be sharply divided into Christians and unbelievers: but they are unlike the children in that they have reached years of discretion and personal choice. The distinctive aim of religious work with youth, therefore, is the adjustment of the subjective life to the religious ideal. This is the one aim of evangelism, and religious work for youth is fundamentally evangelistic. The adjustment in view, however, is not to be regarded as a thing that is achieved by a single act of will, or in a brief time; with a man it may be this, but with a youth it is, normally, a process running through some years. The method of securing it is, therefore, naturally and essentially, educational. Religious work for youth is distinguished from that for the child or the mature Christian by its deliberate evangelistic aim, its purpose to secure personal choice of the religious life; it is distinguished from that for the mature unbeliever by its educational method. It cannot fail to be evangelistic, because it must seek to bring the soul to God in explicit personal choice; it cannot fail to be educational, because the adjustment of the soul which it seeks is an orderly development of an inner capacity for divine fellowship. An education in religion that neglects the need of voluntary, personal determination of spiritual relationships is not suited to youth; neither is an evangelistic method that seeks a short cut to a Christian life. Nothing but a thoroughgoing adjustment of the entire personal life to the divine order can satisfy our ideal. This means that, for youth, the ideals of evangelism and education in religion coalesce.

Elsewhere they are distinct; here they are completely fused. The first principle of religious work for youth is that the evangelistic aim and the educational method are to be blended into one inclusive, far-reaching design.

This being the general aim, there is embraced under it a definite specific aim for each of youth's three periods.

For early adolescence, the specific aim is the assistance of the soul to a distinct, individual, moral character. Religious influences are to help adolescent boys and girls to achieve their freedom, to discover and realize their distinctive individuality. Wherever, in the name of religion, we hinder this process, we are only endeavoring to thwart nature and God. Parents, teachers and pastors on the one hand, and the youth on the other, should come to an explicit understanding that the youth is to have all the freedom that belongs to him, and is to be assisted to it by his religious advisers as fast as he can bear it. The point at which systems of religious education generally break down is their failure,

or inability, to make provision for the
necessary individuation of the soul in youth.
Nothing is more unfortunate than to give
the youth the impression that religion requires him to forego his personal independence. The true educational method will
understand that the day must come when
the young soul, like a new-formed star,
must swing itself free from the mass of
which it has been a part and orb itself into
a separate completeness; and it will pro-
pound as its controlling ideal for the early
years of adolescence the achievement of a
free character, controlled no longer from
without by artificial supports and external
restraints, but from within by a sovereign
law of self-government.

The specific method by which religious
guides are to promote the achievement of a
free character by the youth is a gradual,
though often rapid, relaxation of outward
control accompanied at every step by in-
sistence on self-control. They are to urge
upon the youth his individual responsibility,
and make him bear it in increasing measure.
They are to abjure the tone of authority,

remind the youth that he is not only free but responsible, and urge him, in a friendly and companionable way, to act as a free person and learn to bear the consequences of his own actions. Restraint may still be exercised where the youth is not seriously concerned to claim his freedom; but when he is keenly anxious to take a matter in charge himself and is willing to assume all the responsibility, it is usually a mistake to refuse him the privilege. The teaching of pulpit and classroom should now make clear the requirements of a free life. The youth is to be made to understand that the message of life to him is not a mere invitation to come forth into the broad fields of opportunity and roam at will, but a challenge to come out and try his strength, show what there is of ability and resource in him, see how he can stand up under life's burdens, and meet those tests of skill and readiness and endurance which are not a game but a destiny. Only those are ready for this challenge who have acquired good self-command. The ideal of perfect self-mastery is to shine resplendent

before the eyes of youth. Let him know
that life requires him to be master of himself in fact as well as in name; that self-
government means that he shall be able to
force his blundering hands to acquire skill,
compel his reluctant mind to think and
learn, and hold himself, through weariness
and discouragement, to a steadfast purpose.
If he would be free, let him make sure of
the sufficiency of the law within to govern
him before he casts off the law without.

For the middle period of adolescence, the
distinctive aim of the religious work that
seeks the adjustment of the young person's
life to the divine order should be to equip
him with a stock of religious ideas. This
aim of course runs through all the instruction of earlier and later years; but it is to
stand forth in especial prominence at this
time. With all our emphasis on right teaching, it does not appear that the importance
of the mental period is half realized by religious workers. Professor James has said
that it is difficult to get a new idea into a
man's mind after he is thirty years old; one
may venture the proposition, pedagogical

heresy though it may appear, that it is as
difficult to get an idea, in the same sense of
the word, into the mind of a boy before he
is fifteen. Not that children do not learn,
and remember what they learn ; there is no
disputing the old maxim that the mind of
the child is wax to receive and marble to
retain. But with all their powers of acquisition, just what the children do not acquire
is—ideas. They lay the foundations of
knowledge, they accumulate the materials
and tools to think with. But the work of
thinking out a stock of ideas, that shall be
regulative for the soul through all its future
career, that shall, in fact, constitute one's
mental equipment for life, is performed in
middle adolescence, neither earlier nor later.
We carry through life many impressions received in childhood, but the ideas with which
we live and by which we are controlled to
the end are commonly acquired in the mental period of youth.

Here, then, is the time when the great
truths of the Christian religion are to
be set before the growing mind in their
most stimulating form. Thought is to be

encouraged—independent, unconventional thought; originality is not to be quenched; dogmatism must be banished. But those who would help the youth are to insist that thought shall be thorough, that the mind shall dwell on ideas, not fancies, grasp realities, not dreams, and rest in truths, not half-truths. It is to be considered more important, at this time, to become inured to the work of thinking than to hasten to the conclusions in a wide range of thought. To think one's way through some one question, unraveling all the snarls and putting the matter in right relations on every side, is better than finding out what others have thought about a hundred questions. The struggles with doubt and uncertainty that are so characteristic of this period are nearly always brought on by difficulty with some one point—more often concerning the application of truth to life than concerning the validity of doctrinal truth; and it is the common testimony that to settle one's doubts on the particular points of difficulty usually disposes of them all. For real thought does not go very far until it discovers that any one point leads to every other, so that when one has solved life's meaning in one aspect he has solved it for all.

It is to be a principle with religious guides of youth, that when the mental powers are developing most rapidly they are to be fed with the food of thought, and exercised upon genuine tasks. The defect of much teaching in this period is that it takes all zest and reality out of the tasks of thought by leaning from the first upon a foregone conclusion. The thinking of the fathers, however valid, will not answer for the youth; he is called to work out for himself a respectable set of ideas and beliefs, and it should be real work. The greatest peril of this time is not thought, investigation, even doubt, but the refusal to think, the tolerance that is mere laziness, laying down an argument without pursuing it to the end, the indolence that compromises on agnosticism for lack of energy to think. The personal adjustment of the soul to God is not to be thought of as chiefly an intellectual matter; but man is

morally responsible for the use of his thinking powers, and as an intelligent being is
required to discover for himself a rational
modus vivendi in view of the intelligible
world of truth.

For later adolescence, the specific aim of
religious work should be the adjustment of
personal and social relations. The youth is
now to become an effective social force
within the institutions that make for human
welfare. Every consideration, natural, political, ethical, religious, now calls for the
socialization of his personal power. As he
takes his place in the world, becomes a
factor in the social life of his community,
finds his occupation and life-work, enters
upon the rights and duties of citizenship,
and prepares for those of a new home of
his own, the ranking need and interest
of his spiritual nature is an interpretation
of the social ideal and an enforcement
of its claims upon his capacities for social
service.

The function of religion in this social adjustment of youth is primarily to develop
the Christian social spirit. The social ideal

is the kingdom of God. The meaning of
the organized life of mankind as a progressive realization of God's kingdom is to be
interpreted to youth, and the need of a
religious spirit in the conduct of all human
affairs made clear. The youth is to view
himself as a factor in the world-life whose
value is proportionate to the power of the
Christian spirit of faith and service in him.
He is now to learn that the Christian religion is the great spiritual dynamic for
rendering the organized life of humanity a
blessing to all, and that Christian institutions
are the centers whence this dynamic oper-
ates upon the world.

As one step toward the perfect socialization of the youth as a Christian factor in
the world, religious work aims to secure for
him a felicitous adjustment within the institutions of religion.   In the ideal case, which
is not rare but very common, the youth, having learned to meet individual responsibility
efficiently, and having thought out his personal creed, becomes a member of the church
at the beginning of the social period or
shortly before.   The socialization of his re-

ligious life is the precursor of the adjustments soon to be made to the new social duties of the state and home, and his connection with corporate religion is to furnish inspiration for the effective application of his personality to the tasks that become his portion of the world's work. To secure the identification of the youth with the church, therefore, after he has learned the meaning of personal responsibility and acquired a stock of personal religious convictions, but early in the social period, is to be made a specific aim of religious work.

As we see it, then, the aim of religious work for youth is to secure the complete and harmonious adjustment of the personal life to the divine order; including in this adjustment the intelligent acceptance of personal responsibility for one's life and acts, the acquisition of a well-wrought set of regulative ideas and beliefs, and an effective adjustment of personal power to the demands of social service, both within and without the church. Nothing short of this satisfies or even approaches the ideal for youth; to be satisfied with any lesser aim is to fall below the standard set by the soul of youth itself.

The study of the religious experience of adolescence has also made more clear the expectations that are to be entertained by those engaged in religious work for youth.

To clear the ground of false expectations at the outset: There is no warrant for expecting that children who are religiously minded can always be led up to manhood's faith without periods of doubt and skepticism; or that the religious pathway of youth can always be made smooth and easy; or that anything can take away the uncertainty, turmoil, restlessness and uneasy temper of youth; or that any great number of youth will follow, except in the most general way, any particular course marked out for them; or that anything like uniformity of religious experience for both sexes and all temperaments can be secured; or that souls will be won, in any great numbers, by system; or that any one method or instrumentality can appeal to and satisfy all youth; or that a majority of the youth ought to join the church in early adolescence ; or that any plan or system that may be devised will bring all even of the serious-minded and well-intentioned youth into the church.

But, positively, it is to be expected that religious work, properly conceived and undertaken, will find a powerful ally in the nature of the youth himself. It will count upon nature to further the work of grace in the young heart. The better we understand the soul of youth and the gospel of Christ, the more evident is the fitness of the one for the other. The essential spiritual processes of youth's development, which must represent the Creator's design and intent for the soul, point unmistakably to just such an adjustment of the personal life to the divine will as an enveloping environment as the gospel of Christ seeks to bring about. The blunders of youth in his first use of freedom, his experience with sin, the inevitable discovery of the reaction of his deeds upon himself, show him early his need of a divine Redeemer and Lord. It will surely tend to impart sanity and steadiness to our evangelistic efforts in behalf of young people if it

is understood that it is the part of evangelism to assist nature, not to contravene it.
The soul of the youth is to be formed,
rather than reformed; and even where radical reform is necessary, it is not to be re-
constructed on some other plan than nature's.   There may be a necessary conflict
between nature and grace in the heart of
the mature sinner whose soul has been first
deformed and then ossified in its malforma-
tions, but in youth nothing but unnature
works against the purposes of God's grace.

Accordingly, it is to be expected that nature will provide a proper and sufficient
safeguard for youth's freedom when the
time of estrangement comes.   This is found
in the conscience of the youth himself.   We
have seen that conscience is formed in the
period that precedes the outburst of adolescent life.   The measure of a youth's pros-
pects of success in a free life is the efficiency
of his conscience.   And perhaps the most
reassuring fact among the phenomena of
adolescence is that amid all the storm and
stress, the overturnings and readjustments
of this time, no other feature of the inner

life maintains itself so uncompromisingly as conscience. When the soul puts away the things of childhood, the lessons of elders, the counsels of experience, even its own early ideals and religious faith, conscience still repeats its undeniable "you ought." In dividing itself from all that is not self, the soul finds conscience on the hither side of the line; in all alienation, that is inalienable. It may indeed become hardened by a career of evil-doing, its voice be silenced by repeated disobedience ; but that takes time; in the awakening soul of adolescence, we are to expect to find conscience at its best.

But what is an efficient conscience ? It is not a supersensitive conscience, or a prudish conscience, or a fearful conscience. It is a conscience that makes duty plain, and lays upon one a compelling imperative to perform it. As commonly understood, conscience is both a power of moral discernment and a sense of obligation. The first is its intellectual, the second its moral side. The power of moral discrimination is more or less dependent on one's general intelligence, but the sense of obligation is not thus conditioned. It is the core of the moral nature, the spinal column of the soul. One is strong in the elements of character just in proportion to the strength within him of a compelling sense of personal obligation. Strength of conscience is manifested, not by any finical sensitiveness about doing certain questionable things, but by the vigor and intensity with which one feels his obligation to do the things that are unquestionably good. No external safeguard of any kind, nothing but a miracle, can save a youth if he has no conscience; but if his conscience has been formed aright, and he enters the storm-belt of adolescence with a masterful sense of his personal responsibility, there is no need to fear what the world or the flesh or the devil can do to him.

It is to be expected also that a natural spiritual development will in a few years at longest put a period to the most unpleasant features of youth's estrangement. After the first flush of independence, there comes the time of sober second thought. This is to be anticipated, watched for, planned for.

Religious work is to count upon a real movement of progress toward a less antagonistic spirit and a better mind; it is just possible that fewer youth would be arrested in their development at the point of religious estrangement if they were not so often given to understand that that first step of progress is looked upon as the final one. Spasmodic evangelism attempts to win a self-assertive youth, fails, and gives over the effort with a tone of despair that often makes the youth actually believe that he has sinned away his day of grace. Educational evangelism lets him try his freedom, makes him feel his responsibility, counts on the sobering effect of experience, watches for the appearance of the broader thought and the awakening of the instincts that point to the spirit's reconciliation, and, keeping near him through the whole of this development, never lets him dream that he has finished his course or reached a stopping-place, much less that he is hopelessly lost.

With regard to the fruition, in the social period of youth and later, of religious work conducted on the principles of educational evangelism, it is to be expected, for one thing, that it will result in many Christian characters of the finest type. They cannot be produced by the wholesale, any more than the public schools can make Masters of Arts of all their pupils. But those who come to a Christian manhood or womanhood through a youth in which religious training has always been broadly evangelistic in aim and soundly educational in method should generally be well grounded in the faith, intelligent, with a fine appreciation of spiritual things, efficient in practical service, competent to bear heavy moral burdens and meet the strain of living for God in an unholy world. They are likely to possess a sense of proportion that will restrain them from religious extravaganza, and forbid them also to belittle religion or its just claims. Schooled to the work of the church from the time they are ready for social service, they will be skilful and efficient workers for the Master. And it is chiefly among those whose faith has ripened under this wise and thorough culture that we must look for that depth of conviction without which men and churches may be busy but never prosperous, big but never great, showy but never strong.

A very important fruit to be expected from such religious treatment of youth as we demand is a better temper and attitude toward religion among those who do not come into the church. The sorest charges made against the revival system relate to its effects upon the souls that are turned away from religion, driven into deeper doubt and outright unbelief, taught to become scoffers and mockers, by its methods. If the religion of Christ is presented to the growing soul in accordance with its real needs as they become manifest, it can never appear to that soul a mass of deception, the invention of priests or fanatics, or a thing to be ridiculed and despised. Under the most favorable circumstances, there is every probability that large numbers of men will fail to become professors of religion ; but what temper they shall display toward religion will depend upon the manner in which religious duties and doctrines have been set before them. A large, wise, loving, faithful treatment of the youth by educational methods will leave no such scars upon their spirits in after days as many are disfigured with to-day.

There is warrant also for expecting that such religious work for youth as an educational system with a large evangelistic aim prescribes will contribute largely to the restoration of religion to its rightful preeminence among human concerns. Much is being said of the weakening of the hold of religion upon men, marked by the decay of power in the pulpit, of deep conviction in the pews, of the influence of the church. If religion has lost respect, is it not partly because it has so often been rendered contemptible by its adherents ? Some religious institutions and efforts are despised because they deserve to be. And is not the educational approach to religion—not the intellectual study of religion, but the approach to the whole spiritual concern of man by an ordered and wisely guided development of his inner capacities—the surest remedy for all this ? If religion wants influence, it should have done with haste and intemperate zeal and short cuts and claptrap, cease endeavoring to meet permanent demands by temporary expedients, and go about its work with a breadth of design and a steadiness of purpose worthy of its high claims, and a movement toward its ends that is as unhasting and as unresting as the ongoing of life itself. The displacement of religion from the general educational system of our land, and the failure as yet to provide an adequate, respect-compelling system to supply the lack, go far to explain the degradation of religion from its former prestige among us. To recover such a portion of that prestige as rightfully belongs to it—no one wants it to monopolize attention as it once did—there are several things to be done, but none more effective than to provide for every youth an educational approach to personal religion, a religious training that is everywhere evangelistic in purpose but educational in method, that shapes its expectations year by year in accordance with the work that nature is then doing in the soul, and counts upon the saving grace of God to work along the lines of spiritual development in youth, not against them nor across them. A generation so

trained will not all be church-members, indeed; but they will not hate the church
and despise religion; in their hearts they
will revere both, and worship the God from
whom they come.

CHAPTER X

Agencies and Methods

THOSE who are engaged in Christian work for youth are sometimes repelled and disheartened by the impossible demands made upon them in the name of scientific method. A conception of that work, however, which makes it pursue the evangelistic aim throughout by educational appeals to the naturally unfolding powers of the soul, will go far to fit the scientific demands to the practical situation. Progress will come smoothly where it is agreed, on the one hand, that religious education in the formative years of youth is not to waste precious time in the non-religious study of religion,—the scientific study of the history and philosophy of religion, of ethics and Christian evidences, of the historical and literary criticism of the Bible, and such like subjects, is for later years—on the other hand, that reliance

226

for making disciples of the youth is to be placed chiefly on their educational treatment, not on sentimental influences or emotional appeals.

This conception of religious work for young people has already in fact been widely adopted. It is being discovered that the principles and methods to which the church has been brought by the experience of the last century are in essence identical with the principles and methods to which we are shut up by the psychological and pedagogical requirements of youth. The educational-evangelistic ideal is already implicit in the prevailing conception and organization of religious work; its explicit adoption calls for no overturning of established institutions and no new machinery, but tends rather to simplify our complex ecclesiastical life. For this reason, educational evangelism offers an entirely feasible program for the ordinary church in its work. The agencies and methods required by its principles are already at hand, as we shall quickly see.

There are four chief instruments of education—impression, instruction, association and self-expression. These answer in a general way to the four principal forms of religious exercise, worship, discipleship, fellowship and service; and from the use to be made of these instruments to promote the religious adjustment of the soul to God, the primary principles governing the agencies and methods of religious work for youth may be deduced.

Impressions are the atmosphere of consciousness. Good or bad, they bear the same relation to the health of the mind as the air we breathe bears to that of the body. Of all the instruments of education, they should receive first consideration, because they come first and carry farthest. Bushnell called that period of the child's life before he acquires the use of language the age of impressions, and held it to be the most important time for shaping the child's character by nurture. Sensitiveness to impressions, however, continues throughout childhood, and it is interesting to observe that the experience of infancy in this respect is suggestively repeated in early adolescence.

Like the infant, the youth is without language to express himself. His powers of appreciation develop rapidly, leaving the powers of expression far behind. With only the language of childhood at his command, he is receiving constant revelations of a new realm of life. He can find no words to embody the suggestions, atmospheric notions, hazy ideas that are borne in upon him. No more than the infant, can he tell all that he thinks. No less than the infant, he is busy all the time receiving upon a keenly sensitive soul and recording in an active memory lasting impressions of which at present he gives no sign.

The greatest care is therefore to be exercised to give the youth correct impressions of the Christian life. His impressions are mostly gathered from two sources, the behavior of Christian people, and the public exercises of religion. On the principle of suggestion, they exercise a vast degree of control over thought and conduct where more explicit counsels would be disregarded or forgotten. It is futile to tell a youth that the Christian life is good if he sees that

Christian people find it distasteful, that our faith is full of joy and peace if our actions show anxiety and discontent, that worship is a delight if it is made tedious and irksome, that the church is an institution of divine splendor if it is neglected and despised by the community. No effort is to be spared, on the contrary, to impress the young mind with the sincerity of the faith of Christian people, the strengthening and consoling power which they find in religion, their genuine conviction that he is missing something unspeakably precious if he is not himself living the Christian life. Christian men and women with the eyes of youth upon them must not pose, nor blow the trumpet before them in the streets, but they should take good heed to the impression that their Christian conversation is making.

But the special form of religious exercise that makes largest use of impressions for educational purposes is public worship. To what has already been said of the place of the youth in the services of worship, it is here to be added that these services should give him a harmonious and profound impression of the reality of God and the soul, the power of the spiritual world upon our present, the dignity of duty and the authority of conscience. No other agency can make these impressions as well as the church services. The disastrous fault of some children's religious societies is found in the havoc that they make of the child's more wholesome religious impressions; they seem to make religion a matter of fidgety busyness instead of a simple and beautiful relation of the soul to God. If we look for right impressions, few agencies and simple methods must be the rule. Complexity of religious duties tends to distraction. Everything about public worship, from the style of the building to the announcing of a hymn, is to be given consideration for the impression that it will make on the young mind; and those who are responsible for the exercises of public worship in church, Sunday-school, prayer-meeting and elsewhere, are guilty of disastrous carelessness if they allow lifeless preaching, slovenly praying, fantastic testimony, irreverent and ridiculous singing, or any other such thing, to give the youth a false impression concerning the dignity, beauty, worth and satisfactoriness of the religion of Jesus Christ. Where the religious education of children and youth through their impressions is made a definite object of endeavor, much thought will be given to the worship and the general atmosphere of the Bible school, and great care taken in the conduct of all children's and young people's meetings; the frequent but unforced attendance of the children, and the regular attendance of the youth, at the services of the church will be sought, largely for the sake of the impressions there made; and the arrangement of this service, with its prayers, Scripture, music, offering, sermon and sacrament will be made with the presence of these impressionable young persons in mind.

As an instrument of education, instruction is so important that it has often been identified with education itself. Even where the other instruments are duly recognized, instruction is still made prominent as furnishing the framework for a progressive educational course. An educational evangelism seeks the best possible instruction for the youth. There is no danger of over-intellectualism in religion from insisting that along with the other things involved in the personal adjustment of an intelligent being to a rational Creator, some knowledge in that being of that Creator and his ways is essential. To make a disciple is to make a learner. The effort to devise a course of religious instruction that shall be, year by year, correctly adapted to the needs of the developing soul is to be ardently pursued; and the demand for skilful and efficient instructors deserves attentive heed.

There is no occasion, however, for wasting present opportunities in wistful longing for a curriculum of unattainable pedagogical perfection, or for discouraging the present teaching forces with demands for a kind of skill and efficiency which they do not possess and cannot acquire. The one thing needful is at hand. Because the Bible is a piece of vital literature, it speaks from life to life. The all-important thing is not the course of lessons or the special pedagogical skill of the teacher. It is rather the teach-

er's insight into his work; and a few
simple principles will go far to enable the
average teacher to adapt the vital teachings
of the Bible to the real needs of his pupils.
It is to be his explicit aim to bring the souls
of his class into right relations with the divine order, not by an occasional special
appeal, but by an educational process that
moves forward step by step through a series
of years. In this process, the instruction
given is a conspicuous feature, and its materials and methods are important, but not
so important as the particular object which
the teacher shall set before himself to be
accomplished by any and all means in each
period of his pupil's life.

There are five successive objects to be attained by religious education, and to each of
these in turn the teacher's instruction is to
contribute. With the younger children, the
object is to awaken and enrich the child's
God-consciousness by making him familiar
with the fundamental accounts of God's
ways in nature and with men. With the
children in the acquisitive period, the object
is to impart a knowledge of God's Word;

the Bible, objectively viewed, is the theme, and acquisition the leading interest. Definite lessons are to be assigned and required, and the child should feel that he is making real progress in knowledge. The devotional tone is not to be wanting in such study, but it is easily overworked. The end in view is to get the conscience of the child firmly established upon the objective facts of religious truth and the moral life ; and to this end, his attention is to be fixed upon the objective facts, and seldom diverted to the subjective states or emotions which those facts may rightly enough produce in him. Self-knowledge comes in youth ; now is the time to lay the substantial foundations of knowledge of that which is beyond oneself.

The transition to adolescence calls for a marked change in the specific object of the teacher's work. If the character of his teaching changes as rapidly as the nature of the youth himself, the latter is not likely to think that he has outgrown the Sunday-school. Instruction must now assist him to a free character. During the years of early adolescence, when the soul is developing a moral individuality, instruction is to lay its emphasis on individual ethics. This is the major subject in the ideal course of instruction for this period. Questions of personal conduct are now at the fore. The youth no longer is satisfied to learn, in an objective way, what is right and what wrong; he wants to be led to an insight of his own into moral principles. But he does not want instruction in formal ethics. He prefers lessons from the book of life. Specific, vital instances, developing the principles of conduct by their illustration, are to be dwelt upon and pondered. Biblical biography would therefore seem to furnish the most suitable materials for this period. The study of the lives of the great personalities that move through the pages of Scripture, in the light of the peerless Life there recorded, is the best line to be pursued. Yet the illustration of vital principles of morality is not confined to Biblical characters, and biography is not the only material for teaching and enforcing them. Only let the teacher get the point of view, and conceive the pur-

pose of his instruction to be the assistance
of his pupils to a settlement of their moral
principles in view of divine revelation and
their personal obligations, and he can make
a very unpromising series of lessons serve
his end.

In the period of most rapid mental
growth, interest is likely to pass from moral
principles for the personal life to deeper
questions of general and eternal truth.   Here
again the teaching must change its character as fast as the mind changes its point of
view.   The major subject for the middle
period of adolescence ·is the fundamental
truths of religion.   These are not to be
studied now as in childhood, in a detached
and objective way, as lessons to be learned ;
but the Christian doctrines are to be presented as food for thought, ideas to be
reckoned with in the shaping of one's personal life.   It is even possible now to study
them in some formal, systematic scheme
without making the work repulsive.   Ab-
stract truth, however, attracts but few minds,
young or old ; the natural method of learning a doctrine is to see how it came into

the world and what it meant to those who first apprehended and declared it. Biblical history may therefore be made the medium for the development and exposition of Biblical truth; the history of a thought reveals its bearing on life; and that is what youth wants to know.

The teacher of youth in the social period is to lead them to a knowledge of social ethics, to make them acquainted with the principles of social conduct, the interests and duties that bind men into social, political and ecclesiastical bodies. Now is the time for the study of the kingdom of God as the social ideal foreshadowed in the Old Testament, declared in the New, and being progressively realized in human society through Christian institutions. Biblical history and doctrine are now the background against which are to be set forth the Christian social ideal, the laws of Christian conduct for the organic life of mankind, and the movements of Christian history toward the attainment of this ideal since New Testament times. The claims of the church should now be enforced, along with the religious sanction of the duties of a Christian man to his community, his associates and his family. The history of Christian institutions, past and present, of modern missions and the various benevolent and philanthropic enterprises of our time, especially such as have particular claims upon the young people under instruction, furnish much educational material of value. It must be confessed that the customary treatment of Bible lessons in the ordinary helps shows little appreciation of the need of the young people at this time for an education in social ethics. Yet the teacher who has possessed himself of the idea of religious education for a social being, and has discovered that the kingdom of God is the ruling conception of the Bible from beginning to end, the theme of all the prophets, the end of all historical progress, the one object of the Redeemer's coming, teaching and death, will not suffer for lack of material suitable to make an educational appeal to youth in this period.

From what has been said, it would appear that the proper adaptation of religious in-

struction to growing youth is not so difficult
or hopeless a thing as it has seemed to some.
It is not necessary to adopt revolutionary
methods or wait for an ideal curriculum ; the
main thing has been done when every
teacher has been made to see the definite
object to be accomplished in a given period
and taught to advance from one object to
another as the pupils grow. And in this
connection, the teaching function of the
pulpit is not to be overlooked. It is commonly the pastor's privilege and duty to
lead old teachers and train new ones to this
necessary insight into their work. He is
also to be a teacher of youth. Aside from
special classes of which he may take charge,
he is to count himself the teacher of the
church. There are some things which youth
needs to learn that are better taught from
the pulpit than in the classroom, by sermon
or lecture than by lesson or text-book. The
element of instruction underlies the inspira-
tional and evangelistic features of all true
preaching, and while there is good reason
why the Sunday-schools cannot keep all the
youth in their classes, there is no good rea-

son why the teaching of the pulpit should not appeal to all. Therefore, with a teaching pulpit and an average force of Sunday-school teachers who have been led to understand the dominant interests of the successive periods of childhood and youth, and to watch for the transition from one period to another, there is no reason to despair of the competence of present agencies to cope with the task of the religious instruction of the youth.

The third instrument of education is association. The doctrine of environment has led men to see a new importance in all the surrounding influences that affect human life. It is certainly true that external environment, matters of food, raiment, housing and ventilation, enter into the problems of character-building, and must be duly considered. Nevertheless, nine-tenths of the power of environment over character resides in the personal factors of the environment. In every community, neighborhood or group, there is developed a kind of moral magnetic field of particular character

and well-nigh irresistible power. Whoever
continues long under its influence is assimilated, almost certainly, to the character of
the persons who make it up. But it is important to remember that the really effective personal environment of a youth is
often made up of a very few persons, or
even of one. In the close attachments that
are formed between comrades, classmates,
shopmates and friends, and in the hero worship in which youth indulges so freely, it
often happens that the personality of one
envelops that of the other to the practical
exclusion, for the time, of all other personal
influences; nothing else counts but the influence of this one. Whence it follows that
the entrance into one's field of experience of a single new, forceful personality
may entirely change one's spiritual environment. He may continue to live in the same
home with all the same surroundings, meeting the same companions at work or play,
but his mind and spirit live in a new world
of thought, emotion and purpose furnished
by the new personality. This is the secret
of the almost unbounded power of some

teachers over their pupils, of some pastors over the young people with whom they become really intimate. And this truth is to add hope and zest to efforts in behalf of those whose circumstances are adverse to the attainment of Christian character.

How is the educational power of associations to be most effectively utilized in the promotion of Christian character in the youth? The attempt has been made to guide the associations that young people shall form, and to bring them together in wholesome fellowship under right auspices and good influences, by means of formal religious organizations. The effort has been instructive, and has brought us within sight of the very principle concerning such organizations that is implied in the dominant interests of the successive periods of youth; namely, that formal and established organizations or societies have their place in the social period, but have little power over youth before that period is reached.

In all associations of youth before the social period begins, the sexes are to be kept apart, and the group system followed. The

fellowship of boys and of girls is to be
found, not in any formal organization, but
in natural groups. Of themselves they form
congenial groups, and, as a rule, these groups
formed by natural selection are the best associations possible. Religious work must
take advantage of and cooperate with this
natural disposition of youth to form small
groups of intimates, boys and girls apart.
This way lies success in dealing with them.
Even where the group is not what it ought
to be, it must be accepted as a fact, and it is
seldom wise to try to break it up. If the
gang spirit, with its usual lawlessness, appears, there is indeed something to fear, but
the gang itself may be turned into an effectual educational agency, as has been done
not only by successful settlement workers in
the cities who have had bad gangs to deal
with, but by every Sunday-school teacher
who has known how to develop a good class
spirit in a group of mischievous boys.

It is the especial advantage of the Sunday-school class over every other possible
organization for youth that it usually is one
of these naturally formed groups. More

formal associations have no intrinsic fitness
or attraction for this age ; each group wants
to form its own organization or club.   It is
best to encourage them to do so, and to let
them be as choice of their set, and as exclusive, for the time, as they wish.   The
failure of the Intermediate Endeavor Societies to achieve any success at all commen-
surate with that of the Young People's and
Junior Societies is most instructive here.   It
is not difficult for a competent leader to en-
list large numbers of the younger boys and
girls in a Junior Society; and the young people of social age find a Young People's organization to their mind.   These societies
can be maintained as established features of
a parish organization through many generations of members.   But with those in earlier
and middle adolescence, the case is different.
The Intermediate Society strikes a snag at
once in the difficulty of bringing boys and
girls of this age together for any hearty co-
operation.   Supposing this to be overcome,
most properly by planning separate societies
for the boys and the girls, it is comparatively
easy to form a certain group of them into

the desired organization ; it is their society or club. But it is extremely difficult, in a year or so, to bring the next group into the same organization ; it is not theirs, and they want one of their own. Thus experience leads to the practical conclusion that it is fighting against nature to try to organize the youth of a parish into one inclusive religious association ; the better way is to recognize several little groups ; the organized Sunday-school class is the model religious association for this period.

In this connection the secret of the value of pastors' classes of adolescent boys and girls is apparent. As set features of an educational program, the usefulness of such classes is likely to be limited by formality ; but where a pastor takes one after another of the naturally formed groups of boys and girls into his confidence, and has the tact to be, for a season at least, one of their group, his influence is beyond estimation. He is not likely to use any fixed course of lessons with class after class, for every group needs different treatment. He may aim at definite instruction, or seek to dispose of un-

settled questions and bring the youth to the
personal acceptance of the Christian life;
but his primary object is to put enough of
the right kind of personality into his inter-
course with these young spirits to create for
them a new magnetic field, and thus develop
in them a love for the highest associations.

A few years ago it was discovered that
the Young Men's Christian Associations
were making a mistake by appealing to
young men in the social period largely with
physical apparatus, and since that time
Boys' Departments have been developed by
leaps and bounds, in which boys in the physical period get the advantage of the physical
apparatus of the gymnasium.   The contrary
mistake of depending on social apparatus
to attract youths in the physical period has
been made,—and generally discovered and
abandoned.   But the educational soundness
of the policy of providing some religious
social apparatus for the social period is beyond question.   At about the age when the
High School course is usually completed, the
social impulse asserts itself, the sexes begin
to discover their common interests, and a

large class draws together with a common spirit. A little later, the smaller groups are scattered as the young people leave school and seek employment in new fields, often away from home; where there has been exclusiveness or clannishness, it must now in the course of nature disappear or lose much of its force. The natural line of development now calls for the association of individuals in larger and more formal organizations; hence the established, inclusive Young People's Society is now in place. What kind of Society it shall be; whether it shall be chiefly concerned with religious meetings or with practical good works; whether it shall aim to include all the young people of the parish in a social organization or only the more devout in a united effort at spiritual improvement; whether membership in it shall be regarded as a step toward church-membership or its members be chiefly those who are already communicants; whether it shall represent a training school for young people in religious work or a specialized department of religious work in behalf of young people; whether,

in some fields, a separate society for the
young people apart from the other parish
organizations is needful;—these and many
such questions are to be decided in view of
the special circumstances in each parish.
But nothing can excuse the failure to offer
youth in the social period the opportunity
to form those associations with others of
their own age which go so far to establish
Christian character and develop personal
usefulness in the service of God.

The fourth instrument of education is
self-expression. This also has its use in
effecting the adjustment of a young person
to the divine order. Just what that use
shall be, depends upon the person. The one
thing certain is that system and formality
are practically impossible in this matter.
Certain forms of religious self-expression
are to be suggested as usual and fitting,
but never prescribed, much less enforced.
Youth rebels against the usual and the conventional, because what it needs is some
unique self-expression to promote the development of a new self. The religious self-

expression of youth is for this reason to be largely self-originated and wholly self-chosen. We have seen that differences of temperament and sex profoundly affect the experiences through which youths have to pass; it is also to be observed that they modify the manner of self-expression even more than the form and intensity of the experience. Even with identical experiences, persons of different temperaments will express themselves in radically different ways; and when the experiences themselves are so widely different as almost to preclude mutual understanding, it is futile indeed to prescribe certain forms of self-expression as the proper and desirable ones for all.

Very little religious self-expression is to be looked for in early adolescence, or before. This is not a time for expression but for reception and appreciation; self-discovery is to precede self-revelation. The special religious activities that are now expressive and educational are confined chiefly to private prayer, study and thought upon religious themes, and attendance at public services, without, however, being required to commit or express oneself very definitely. But the intense physical vigor of the period points to the need of special effort to get the conception of religious obligation expressed in the performance of the common duties of life; religious motives are best manifested by self-control, and the glad and faithful performance of the work that is the present duty.

The expression of one's beliefs, convictions and experiences in language may properly be attempted, in a cautious and tentative way, in the middle period of adolescence; as the thoughts and convictions become clear and settled, the expression of them should become definite and positive. Yet this is the time to guard against self-conceit and censoriousness; and the best self-expression is the effort, which ought to meet with steadily increasing success, to bring one's own actions into somewhat nearer accord with one's ideals. In the social period, religious self-expression comes most naturally through some form of social service. The time has arrived for the cultivation of religious fellowship, the exchange of experiences and testimony for the mutual strengthening of an associated body of worshipers, the expression of one's participation in the common religious life through the medium of common prayer. It is to be remembered, however, that the educational value of any form of self-expression is now precisely equivalent to its social value; the educational benefit to be derived from giving testimony in a prayer-meeting, for instance, is neither greater nor less than the good to be done by such testimony to those who hear. If some other form of religious self-expression is more useful, it is more educational. Young people of this period are to be enlisted in united Christian enterprises for the accomplishment of practical good. They are to find out without further delay, by practical experience, what service they can best render to the kingdom, and to discipline themselves for the greatest possible effectiveness in their chosen lines of religious work.

When our Lord stood by the grave of Lazarus and called him back to life, "he that was dead came forth, bound hand and foot with grave-clothes; and his face was bound about with a napkin." And the Lord bade those about him, "Loose him, and let him go."

Youth also is a resurrection. The child has died, and the youth comes wonderingly forth upon life, conscious that the garments that were his necessity hitherto are fetters now, and that his face is covered with a heavy veil. And the Lord's command to those who stand about with loving eagerness to be of service to him is just, "Loose him, and let him go."

The defenses and restraints with which we tenderly surround the child are hindering grave-clothes to the youth, to be worn only in contravention of the divine command. Our first religious duty to the youth is to throw him on his own responsibility. No doubt it is a dangerous thing to do,— let us be cautious; it opens the door for a life of sin,—let us be warned. But it is necessary,—let us be reconciled; it is natural,—let us take courage; and divinely ordered,—let us have faith.

But can we let him go, and trust him to a free life, without some explicit pledge that he will make that life Christian ? When and where and how does the educational method expect to secure that decisive act of will by which a young person becomes a Christian ? What of decision days, pledges and self-consecrations ? We have written to little purpose if we have not yet made it plain that the appeal to the will is implicit in all the work of educational evangelism from first to last ; but we have written to little purpose if we have not also made it plain that the object of educational evangelism is not to secure one critical act of will, but to guide all acts of will ; and more than that, to shape and determine for God and the right the entire spiritual life of which the will is only a part. As the soul, like a flower of many petals, unfolds at the impulse of enlarging life, the religious education of the will should proceed along with the religious development of the entire spiritual nature. The inner life in all its aspects, mental, emotional and volitional, is to be shaped for God as a unit ; a life so formed will surely confess its God in its own convincing way. The aim is not so much to secure a particular kind of confession at a given time as to make sure that some genuine confession must come some time.

It is indeed to be expected that there will be, in every community or parish, some prevailing way of making the first confession. It is surely imperative that there shall always be before the youth some simple, recognized mode of signifying the purpose to live a Christian life and the desire to enter the fellowship of the church; no such purpose or desire should be allowed to go unexpressed for lack of opportunity and encouragement to make it known. The simplest and most natural method of expression, the one most consonant with the character, tastes, traditions and religious surroundings of the individual, is the best. This for some is to rise for prayers in a public meeting, or to take a stand at a revival service, or to sign a pledge card, perhaps on a Sunday-school decision day, or on coming into a Young People's Society; but there is nothing else

so good as the simple personal avowal made
in conversation with a friend, parent, teacher
or pastor, to be followed at the fitting time
by a public confession of faith.

The meaning of this public confession, too,
is to be interpreted to the youth, for it is
widely misconceived. It is very properly
associated with reception into the church.
But too many look upon this as the final
step, the attainment of the spiritual goal.
To confess Christ and be received into the
church is to them the end of religious development; the faith which they acknowledge represents a finished creed; they enter
the fellowship of the saints, who have been
washed clean from all sin, have attained the
Christian character, among whom none unworthy is allowed to enter. Many a youth,
because of this view, holds himself long
aloof from church-membership, counting
himself unworthy; and many another, entering in, is sorely disappointed to find the
church itself imperfect and the heights of
spiritual attainment still far above him.

Very different is the idea of membership in
the church set forth in the New Testament.

It is indeed to be without spot or wrinkle or
any such thing; but its glory is its Head,
not its members.   Those who enter it are
called to be saints; but their saintliness is
not in perfection attained, but in perfection
pursued as they follow the perfect Christ.
The earthly church is not for those who have
attained, but for those who press on; not
for those already made perfect, but for all
penitent sinners, that they may be cleansed
of their sin; not for those only who are wise
in the ways of God, but for his inexperienced
children who would learn his ways; not for
those alone whose virtue is established, but
for evil-doers who are learning to do well;
not a university for those who have taken
one or more degrees for religious achievement, but a common school where all God's
children are to be taught his service; not a
select company of those in whom the image
of the Master is especially displayed, but a
host of those who are loyal to his ideals,
though they follow them faintly and afar
off.   Its door should open easily to the faint-
est and most timid knocking; for it is
God's Church, instituted by him for the bless-

ing of his lowliest and weakest children;
Christ's Church, where publicans and harlots
are welcome when they leave their sin to go
with him. The youth is not to be suffered
to believe that he is not eligible to enter the
church until he has attained his ideals of
Christian character, nor that when he enters the education of his spirit is all complete; the church is given him as a divine
assistant to aid him in a lifelong quest of
truth, and worth, and God.

And what of those, numerous in every
community, who have reached mature years
and gone the way of sin? Educational
evangelism recognizes the need of special
efforts in their behalf, which make use of
other than educational means. It would say
little of these efforts, save only that they
are special, and should not be deemed necessary for the majority. It would assist them
by laying the right foundation for character
in these wanderers before they go astray, by
suggesting methods based upon the necessary differences in the experiences through
which different men must go on their way
to the kingdom, and by pointing out the

educational value of the experience of life,
the sobering effects of his career upon the
sinner, the waning or passing, in all except
abnormal persons, of the youthful passions
and ambitions which are the commonest occasion for a life of sin, and which, when
they are exhausted, leave the soul empty for
a divine infilling. The evangelism that relies upon educational methods does not claim
the whole field; its especial sphere is youth;
yet it remembers that life itself is education;
it expects the long years that commonly in-
tervene between youth and death to do
something for the soul, more especially if it
has wandered far; it looks for men to
advance in knowledge and grace, in all
spiritual wisdom and understanding, in all
virtue and Christlikeness, as they advance
in years, and counts their educational discipline ended only on the day of their assumption to the heavenly kingdom, where
faith is changed for sight, prophecy for ful-
filment, and the soul's possibilities for complete realization at last.

In conclusion, the working principles to

which our study leads may be conveniently summed up in the following theses of educational evangelism; if compression gives them the appearance of dogmatism, it is a fault of the form, not of the spirit.

1.   The Spirit of God finds his way into human lives along the lines of educational development; regeneration comes by education as often as any other way.

2.   The natural order of the soul's development in youth is first the achievement of personal freedom, then the discovery of the meaning and unity of life, and finally a reconciliation and adjustment to the divine order, including one's earthly place and lot; these stages overlap, but are not to be confused; they take time, and are not to be artificially cut short; they come to a natural end, when the special opportunity presented by each is forever past.

3.   Religious work for youth is to be planned and carried on in harmony with this order of development, not at cross purposes with it.

4.   Religious work for youth should therefore pursue the evangelistic aim—the

right adjustment of the personal life to the divine order, by the educational method— the orderly development of the soul's capacities for God.

5. The specific aim of religious work for the early period of adolescence is to promote the achievement of a free, individual, moral character, responsive to religious motives; the specific method is that of steadily increasing the range of the youth's definite responsibility, with constant appeal to his sense of personal obligation to God.

6. Conscience is the one effectual safeguard of freedom, all external supports and restraints being futile without it.

7. On the principle of suggestion, the impressions made in childhood and early youth go far to shape religious thought and conduct through life.

8. The specific aim for the middle period of adolescence is to equip the soul with a stock of religious ideas and beliefs.

9. The doctrines of the Christian faith furnish an ideal educational stimulus when offered to the youthful mind to be exam-

ined, pondered and assimilated point by point, rather than as incontestable verities to be accepted in bulk.

10.   The discipline of doubt is not to be feared so much as the indolence that declines to think.

11.   The specific aim of religious work in the third period of youth is to secure the social adjustment of the individual life within the religious body.

12.   The commanding ideal for this age is the kingdom of God, the social ideal of humanity, to be progressively realized through the Christian home, church, state and other institutions.

13.   The instruction to be offered youth is to be governed by the specific aims above mentioned ; in the early period, it is to center about individual ethics and personal responsibility ; in the second, about the truths of the faith and personal creeds ; in the third, about social and institutional religion and the place of the individual in the social whole.

14.   Suitable materials for the effective education of the spirit at every stage of de-

velopment are found in the vital literature of the Bible.

15. The appeal of the Divine Personality is to be presented to the soul at every stage in accordance with its major interests at the time; the direction and tone of this appeal being more important for the grading of religious educational work than the materials or methods to be used.

16. The place of the youth is in the church itself; but it is better that that place should be quite undefined, requiring no confessions or obligations, but affording stimulus for thought and growth.

17. The power of environment over character rests chiefly in its personal factors, and one strong personality may alter the entire character of a youth's effective spiritual environment.

18. Children are not, as a rule, to be received into the church, or confirmed, until their free individual characters are formed and their personal creeds thought out; that is not, ordinarily, before their sixteenth year.

19. Previous to the social period, youths

are to be dealt with either as individuals or in naturally formed groups, not in large bodies.

20. Established organizations, formal societies, and the like, are chiefly effective after the beginning of the social period, and count for little before that time.

21. The experiences through which youth pass, and, still more decidedly, the forms of expression which they will adopt, are profoundly affected by both temperament and sex; and this precludes all possibility of a uniform system of religious development.

22. The expression of the religious life of youth is to be sought in self-initiated or self-chosen forms of activity, rather than in established and conventional forms; what is wanted is self-activity and self-expression to promote self-development.

23. No possible method or system can bring all into the Christian life in youth, or dispense with the necessity for the conversion of mature men.

24. The education of a human spirit is never complete until, at whatever age, the

free personality is brought at last into happy reconciliation with his Father.

25.   The common experiences of mature life in the free world are divinely ordered with a view to that final reconciliation.